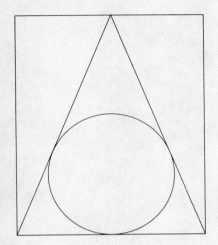

# Notwith-standing My Weakness

## Neal A. Maxwell

Deseret Book Company
Salt Lake City, Utah
1981

Library of Congress Catalog Card Number 81-65352
ISBN 0-87747-855-4

Printed in the United States of America
10    9    8    7

## Dedication

To the "true believers in Christ" (4 Ne. 1:36) who continue to serve Him notwithstanding their weaknesses—who will, when His history is written, be the real heroes and heroines of our age. Meanwhile, these seemingly ordinary souls—weak and foolish in the eyes of the world—are all about us, keeping the commandments, receiving the ordinances, doing their duties, enduring "valiantly for the gospel of Jesus Christ" (D&C 121:29), and "always abounding in good works" (Ether 12:4).

# Contents

# Acknowledgments

Deep appreciation is expressed to readers Elizabeth Haglund, Jeffrey Holland, Bruce Hafen, Roy W. Doxey, and James Jardine—who are not responsible for what follows but who have made it more responsible.

Special gratitude is due Jeananne Gruwell Hornbarger for her patient processing of words and drafts and in such a congenial way.

Lowell Durham, Jr., and Eleanor Knowles, once again, were encouragers as well as editors to whom thanks are gladly and deservedly given.

Finally, to my wife, Colleen, loving gratitude for suggesting the title and the focus of the book, an effort that she thought I might attempt—notwithstanding my weaknesses, which she experiences more than any other mortal.

# 1

## *Notwithstanding My Weakness*

In a kingdom where perfection is an eventual expectation, our feelings of anxiety and inadequacy should not surprise us. Just as earlier disciples were anxious and even "astonished" as Jesus taught certain demanding doctrines (Mark 10:28), so today there is really no way present prophets can describe where we must yet go without creating a sense of distance. We are not merely journeying next door or even across town.

While this sense of inadequacy has its uses, conscientious Christians—not the slackers or the falsely secure—whose devotion has been declared in dozens of ways deserve and need some encouragement and reassurance. To such individuals, the counsel is clearly not, "You've got it made," "Take it easy," "Be casual." Rather, it is: "You're headed in the right direction"; "You're doing better than you know"; "Look back, just for a moment, and see how far you've come"; "Do you see those distant lights, even dimly, for they are the lights of the City of God"; "Do not weary or let the adversary deflect you now."

This precious perspective, which features the *feasibility* of our quest, must not be lost in the midst of our anxieties and stresses.

Church doctrines and Church duties are essential to our personal progress, but also to the retention of this reassurance. We can, for instance, cope with the challenges of continuing our journey notwithstanding our weakness if we truly focus on the two great, overarching commandments on which hang all the law and the prophets. Moreover, we will find sooner or later that we must believe in the whole of His gospel—not just the portions that please us.

Likewise, in these times of hopelessness we must cultivate in ourselves a particularized and "perfect brightness of hope." We will surely need, too, genuine patience, not only with others but also with *ourselves*, with a divine process, for impatience so often opens the door for despair and contempt.

Furthermore, even though the world worsens and coarsens, we can, notwithstanding, proceed with our Lord-given task of putting off the natural man and becoming saint-like. Simultaneously, though we feel weak, our help is much needed by those hundreds of thousands of converts coming into the Church who will be undertaking the very same "mighty change" in their hearts and lives.

As together we become less spotted by the world and more pure—achieving this condition in a time of gross immorality and corruption—then we can become worthy of being called "true believers in Christ."

All these things and more can be done notwithstanding our weaknesses, if we are willing to push on in a brisk, but *paced*, way, remembering always that the Church is the Lord's learning center into which have been "gathered of every kind." Not only are we very much aware, therefore, of our own weaknesses, but we are also aware of each others'.

Perceptive Jethro had plenty of data to back up the loving but crisp counsel he gave so directly to his remarkable son-in-law, Moses. (See Exodus 18.) Even prophets notice their weaknesses. Nephi persisted in a major task, "notwithstanding my weakness." (2 Nephi 33:11.) Another Nephite prophet, Jacob, wrote candidly of his "overanxiety" for those with whom he was not certain he could communicate adequately. (Jacob 4:18.)

President Spencer W. Kimball has had those telling moments when he has felt as if he simply could not meet certain challenges. Yet he did and he does.

Given our weaknesses, however, paced progress is essential, much as God used six measured and orderly creative periods (followed by respite) in preparing man and this earth. There is a difference, therefore, between being steadily and effectively or "anxiously" engaged, on the one hand, and, on the other hand, being frantically engaged one moment and being passive and detached the next.

Lest we wrongly assume that traveling on the straight and narrow path requires hectic pace, let us remember that the Lord *does not* want us to weary by the way and for very good reasons. Thoughtless haste and spurts of service are not what is desired, for such naiveté is like the businessman who confuses volume with profit.

The Lord has clearly indicated His concern for us if we are weary; He has even given us counsel on sleep to avoid that weariness and in order to be vigorous: ". . . cease to sleep longer than is needful; retire to thy bed early, that ye may not be weary; arise early, that your bodies and your minds may be invigorated." (D&C 88:124.)

Moreover, for centuries there has been the vital law of the Sabbath to provide us rest from our regular labors (or at

least an appropriate and approved change in the way we
expend our energies)—from temporal labors to the more
spiritual activities of the Sabbath.

The Savior, no stranger to pressure and to weariness,
has ever been mindful of His flock.

Happily, we have had preserved for us, through the
writings of Mark, an episode in which the press of the
crowd was so great on the Savior and His disciples that
there was "no leisure so much as to eat." (Mark 6:30-32.) It
was, therefore, the Savior's desire to take His disciples pri-
vately by ship to a desert place, so that they could obtain
much-needed respite, illustrating that where the pace is
brisk and people are giving much and constantly, a time of
refreshing and renewal is needed.

Much is left to us, however, as to the development of
wisdom concerning our labors—even the labors we perform in behalf of the Lord. The counsel the Lord gave the
Prophet Joseph Smith in the midst of his urgent and high-
priority task of the translation of the Book of Mormon is
worthy of our contemplation: "Do not run faster or labor
more than ye have strength and means . . . but be diligent
unto the end." (D&C 10:4.) If such counsel was appropriate
for the Lord to give to a *conscientious* young prophet with regard to the translation of the vital Book of Mormon (which
of necessity had to precede so many subsequent and great
events such as the long-awaited restoration of the Church,
the priesthood, and various keys), then surely that same
counsel can be appropriately applied to some of the lesser
tasks you and I undertake in the Church. The Lord wants
us to be *diligent but prudent*. We are not to give our cross a
hurried heft merely to see if we can lift it and then put it
down—we are to carry it for the balance of our lives. And
pace matters very much. The pioneers crossed the plains in

a paced way, arriving weary but intact—a lesson for us all!

Striking the proper balance is one of the keenest tests of our agency. Therefore, we need to ask regularly for inspiration in the use of our time and in the making of our daily decisions. So often our hardest choices are between competing and desirable alternatives (each with righteous consequences), when there is *not* time to do both at once. Indeed, it is at the mortal intersections—where time and talent and opportunities meet—that priorities, like traffic lights, are sorely needed. Quiet, sustained goodness is the order of heaven, not conspicuous but episodic busyness.

Thus the counsel the Lord gave the Prophet Joseph Smith is clearly worthy of our contemplation. In the decade of preparation (the 1820s), the Lord did not have the Prophet engaged in thirty-six other projects. He focused the Prophet's energies and strength on that very basic and fundamental task, the translation of the Book of Mormon, and, even so, counseled prudent diligence.

There were other very urgent tasks that the Lord needed the Prophet Joseph Smith to do later. Yes, the Prophet finally gave *all* that he had, but his contribution to the work of the Lord was not in a single project; it was spread over many high priority projects and also over a period of time. The paced performance of Joseph Smith brought results that were to touch millions! We, too, may be ready to give our all, but it is usually not required in one lump sum.

While it should never surprise us to see prophets preaching the same doctrines and giving the same counsel, it is always interesting and pleasing to note the parallels. Such congruence is very apparent with regard to the aforecited counsel the Lord gave the Prophet Joseph Smith concerning his labors in translating the Book of Mormon and that given by King Benjamin to his people. Having urged Church members to be diligent in doing their specific and recurring duties, such as imparting of their substance to the poor, King Benjamin then gave this wise counsel:

"And see that all these things are done *in wisdom and order*; for it is *not requisite* that a man should run faster than he has strength. And again, it is expedient that he should be *diligent*, that thereby he might win the prize; therefore, *all things must be done in order.*"(Mosiah 4:27. Italics added.)

Running faster than we have strength "is not requisite." Doing things diligently but "in wisdom and order" is, in fact, necessary if one is to "win the prize." This balance between pace and diligence is a high and demanding exercise in the use of our time, talent, and agency. It is easy to be passive and withdrawn. In some ways it is likewise easy to fling ourselves thoughtlessly and heedlessly into a task that we then do not continue as we commenced. (See D&C 9:5.)

It takes, however, real wisdom, discipline, and judgment to do things in order. Only then do we "win the prize." True effectiveness requires the help of heaven, which is given only under certain conditions. The "dignity of causality" that attends genuine accomplishment is a result of *diligence with dignity* as we labor to bring about that accomplishment.

We need that same sense of inspired priority and the same kind of balance and pace. When our pace exceeds our strength and means, the result is prostration instead of sustained dedication. Directions on such matters can be and are given to us through the process of private inspiration, just as they were given to the Prophet Joseph Smith as he labored so diligently to translate the Book of Mormon, so that all of us could be nourished thereby.

A few little flowers will spring up briefly in the dry gulley through which torrents of water pass occasionally. But it is steady streams that bring thick and needed crops. In the agriculture of the soul that has to do with nurturing attributes, flash floods are no substitute for regular irrigation.

Pace, which requires diligent, sustained effort, is not the way of those who fling themselves into a single task and quickly become depleted and, therefore, cannot help again for a season. Church service is not a breathlessly-brought-about roadshow followed by detached repose!

Paul counseled us to be instant in season and out of season (2 Timothy 4:2), or as some translations compositely render, "keep at it in both troublesome and favorable seasons." Steady devotion is better than periodic exhaustion, or as President Spencer W. Kimball has said, "Keep moving." Even rigorousness has its rhythm.

Without balance and pace, therefore, our weaknesses become even more pronounced, causing some of us who would not chastise a neighbor for his frailties to have a field day with our own. Some of us stand before no more harsh a judge than ourselves, sometimes dealing more justly with others than with ourselves. (See Ether 10:11.) Pace is so essential to personal progress lest we magnify our weaknesses instead of our callings.

The need for pace even though brisk should not offend our senses when we read this counsel from the Lord: "And ye cannot bear all things now; nevertheless, be of good cheer for I will lead you along." (D&C 78:18; see also D&C 50:40.)

Moving from considerations of pace to our need to proceed forward notwithstanding our weaknesses, we can use the scriptures as a developmental display window through which we can see gradual growth in others that should help us and encourage us. Enoch's unique people were improved "in process of time." (Moses 7:21.) Jesus "received not of the fulness at the first, but received grace for grace" (D&C 93:12), and even He grew and "increased in wisdom and stature" (Luke 2:52).

In the scriptural display window we see Lehi struggling as an anxious and "trembling parent." (2 Nephi 14.) We see sharp, sibling rivalries but also deep friendships like that of David and Jonathan. We see that all conflict does not end in catastrophe. We view, though through glass darkly, misunderstandings even in rich relationships like that of Paul and Barnabas. We see a prophet candidly reminding a King Saul grown proud that there was a time when "thou wast little in thine own sight." (1 Samuel 15:17.)

We see our near-perfect parents, Adam and Eve, coping with genuine challenges in their first family, for their children, too, came trailing traits from their formative first estate.

We see a legalistic Paul, but later read his matchless sermon on charity. (See 1 Corinthians 13.) We see a jailed John the Baptist—and there had been "no greater prophet" (Matthew 11:11)—nevertheless needing reassurance (Matthew 11:2-4). We see Peter walking bravely but briefly on water, but then requiring rescue from Jesus' outstretched hand (Matthew 14:25-31); later we see a majestic Peter stretching forth his strong hand to Tabitha after helping to restore her to life (Acts 9:36-46).

Moroni was not, we learn, the first underinformed Church leader to conclude erroneously that another leader was not doing enough. (See Alma 60.) Nor was Pahoran's sweet, generous response to his "beloved brother," Moroni, the last such that will be needed. (Alma 61.)

Thus we see in the scriptures many examples of spiritual growth notwithstanding the initial weaknesses of these exemplars.

What else can we do to manage these vexing feelings of inadequacy? Are there specific remedies for these general feelings?

1. We can distinguish more clearly between divine discontent and the devil's dissonance, between dissatisfaction with self and disdain for self. We need the first and must shun the second, for when conscience calls to us from the next ridge, it is not solely to scold but also to beckon.

2. We can contemplate how far we have already come in the climb along the pathway to perfection; it is usually much further than we acknowledge, and such reflections restore resolve. True, we *are* still "unprofitable servants," but partly because when "we have done that which was our duty to do" (Luke 17:10), with every ounce of such obedience comes a generous bushel of blessings.

3. We can accept help as well as gladly give it. Happily, General Naaman received honest but helpful feedback, not from fellow generals, but from his orderlies. (See 2 Kings 5:1-14.) In the economy of heaven, God does not send thunder if a still, small voice is enough, or a prophet if a priest can do the job.

4. We can make allowance more than we sometimes do for the agency of others (including our children). Often our best effort is not fully effectual because of someone else's worst effort.

5. We can write down (rather than muse upon) and then act upon a few of those otherwise transient resolutions for self-improvement that are like a pebble in one's shoe.

6. We can honestly acknowledge, in those moments of wonderment about our mattering, that if we were to die

today, we would be genuinely and deeply missed. Perhaps parliaments would not praise us, but no human circle is so small that it does not touch another circle and another and another.

7. We can put our hand to the plow, looking neither back nor around, comparatively. Our opportunities as well as our gifts differ; some are more visible and impactful. The historian Moroni felt inadequate as a writer beside the mighty Mahonri Moriancumer, who wrote overpoweringly. We all have *at least* one gift *and* an open invitation to seek "earnestly the best gifts." (D&C 46:8. Italics added.)

8. We can make quiet but more honest inventories of our strengths. Most of us are dishonest bookkeepers and need confirming "outside auditors." He who in the first estate was thrust down delights in having us put ourselves down. Self-contempt is of Satan; there is none of it in heaven. We should, of course, learn from our mistakes, but without forever viewing the instant replays lest these become the game of life itself.

9. We can add to each other's storehouse of self-esteem by giving deserved, specific commendation more often. We should remember, too, that those who are breathless from going the second mile need deserved praise just as the fallen need to be lifted up.

10. We can also keep moving. Crosses are easier to carry when we keep moving. Men finally climbed Mount Everest, not by standing at its base in consuming awe, but by shouldering their packs and by placing one foot in front of the other. Feet are made to move forward.

11. We can know that when we have *truly* given what we have, it is like paying a full tithe; it is, in that respect, *all* that was asked. There are situations in which we are like the widow who cast in her two mites; what we contribute

in talents may seem but little as others give of their "abundance," but we have actually given of our "penury." (See Luke 21:1-44.)

12. We can allow for the reality that God is still more concerned with growth than with geography. Those who marched in Zion's Camp were not exploring the Missouri countryside, but their own possibilities.

13. We can learn that at the center of our agency is our freedom to form a healthy attitude toward whatever circumstances we are placed in. Those, for instance, who stretch themselves in service, though laced with limiting diseases, are often the healthiest among us. The strong Spirit *can* drive weak flesh beyond where the body first agrees to go!

14. Finally, we can accept this stunning, irrevocable truth: Our Lord can lift us from deep despair and cradle us midst any care. We cannot tell Him *anything* about either aloneness *or* nearness.

This is a gospel of grand expectations, but God's grace is sufficient for each of us if we remember that there are no *instant* Christians.

Furthermore, when we contemplate how the Lord has said that He would use the foolish, the weak, the despised, the simple, the unlearned to do His work, this is bound to produce in us certain feelings that must, therefore, be placed in the proper perspective.

*First* of all, we are bound to feel weak and foolish in relation to Him whose work this is.

*Second*, we will sometimes appear to be weak and foolish in terms of the criteria the world uses to measure wisdom and strength. "For the preaching of the cross is to them that perish foolishness; but unto us which are saved it is the power of God." (1 Corinthians 1:18.) As irreligion be-

comes the secular religion, it will be even more so. But the
contempt of the world has its uses, too.

The Lord has declared, time and time again, His inten-
tions to use such individuals *in spite* of how the world feels
about them:

> But God hath chosen the foolish things of the world to confound
> the wise; and God hath chosen the weak things of the world to con-
> found the things which are mighty. (1 Corinthians 1:27.)

> The weak things of the world shall come forth and break down the
> mighty and strong ones. (D&C 1:19.)

> To prepare the weak for those things which are coming on the
> earth, and for the Lord's errand in the day when the weak shall con-
> found the wise, and the little one become a strong nation. . . . And by
> the weak things of the earth the Lord shall thrash the nations by the
> power of his Spirit. (D&C 133:58-59.)

> That the fulness of my gospel might be proclaimed by the weak
> and the simple unto the ends of the world, and therefore kings and rul-
> ers. (D&C 1:23.)

> Wherefore, I call upon the weak things of the world, those who are
> unlearned and despised, to thrash the nations by the power of my spir-
> it. (D&C 35:13.)

Lest we resist even inwardly being so described, let us
remember how noble are some who are included: "Verily,
thus saith the Lord unto you, my servant Joseph Smith, . . .
I raised you up, that I might show forth my wisdom
through the weak things of the earth." (D&C 124:1.)

*Third*, we will also feel foolish because we are very conscious of our own actual weaknesses. Indeed, the Lord has
even indicated that He will bring our weaknesses vividly to
our attention:

> Nevertheless, the Lord God *showeth us our weakness* that we may
> know that it is by his grace, and his great condescensions unto the chil-
> dren of men, that we have power to do these things. (Jacob 4:7. Italics
> added.)

And if men come unto me I will *show* unto them their weakness. *I give unto men weakness* that they may be humble; and my grace is sufficient for all men that humble themselves before me; for if they humble themselves before me, and have faith in me, then will I make weak things become strong before them. (Ether 12:27. Italics added.)

It should give us some consolation to know, however, that other disciples (far more advanced than we) have had some of these same feelings. Paul, in addition to his thorn in the flesh, apparently was not impressive in terms of his physical appearance. Like us, he noticed that others noticed: "For his letters, say they, are weighty and powerful; but his bodily presence is weak, and his speech contemptible." (2 Corinthians 10:10.)

Apparently Paul's style of speech was not highly regarded either. "But though I be rude in speech, yet not in knowledge. . . . " (2 Corinthians 11:6.)

Hyrum Smith, just hours before he was murdered, had been reading this reassuring verse about others noticing and reacting uncharitably to our weaknesses:

And it came to pass that the Lord said unto me: If they have not charity it mattereth not to thee, thou hast been faithful; wherefore, thy garments shall be made clean. And because thou hast seen thy weakness thou shalt be made strong, even unto the sitting down in the place which I have prepared in the mansions of my Father. (Ether 12:37.)

Our serenity, like Hyrum's, need not depend entirely on the charity of others regarding our weaknesses. Our weaknesses bring compensatory blessings. On one occasion the Lord said of the Prophet Joseph, "I have sent forth the fulness of my gospel by the hand of my servant Joseph; and in weakness have I blessed him." (D&C 35:17.)

Even when there is unbelief and guilt, if we will trust

Him, then another encouraging promise is in force for us just as it was for earlier members of the Church:

> But now I tell it unto you, and ye are blessed, not because of your iniquity, neither your hearts of unbelief; for verily some of you are guilty before me, but I will be merciful unto your weakness.
>
> Therefore, be ye strong from henceforth; fear not, for the kingdom is yours. (D&C 38:14-15.)

The Lord has also clearly promised to succor us in the midst of our temptations: "Behold, and hearken, O ye elders of my church, saith the Lord your God, even Jesus Christ, your advocate, who knoweth the weakness of man and how to succor them who are tempted." (D&C 62:1.) Such divine, close-in support as is promised in the scriptures means that God's grace will be sufficient for us if we are humble.

However, we must turn ourselves over to the Lord, so that we can be succored by Him and so that our weaknesses can even become strengths.

It is also required of us, however, that we help others along the way. The counsel given to Frederick G. Williams when he was called to be a counselor in the First Presidency applies to us all: "Wherefore, be faithful; stand in the office which I have appointed unto you; succor the weak, lift up the hands which hang down, and strengthen the feeble knees." (D&C 81:5.)

Those are second-commandment duties. Job was praised for doing them: "Behold, thou hast instructed many, and thou hast strengthened the weak hands. Thy words have upholden him that was falling, and thou hast strengthened the feeble knees." (Job 4:3-4.)

Clearly, we are to help each other in the journey along the straight and narrow path. Even though such helping seems to drain us of energy and surely takes precious time, it will actually strengthen us. We will become more like Him whose followers we are.

When we misbehave, however, we disappoint the weak (each other) and become a stumbling block. Paul was sensitive to this:

> But take heed lest by any means this liberty of yours become a stumblingblock to them that are weak.
>
> For if any man see thee which hast knowledge sit at meat in the idol's temple, shall not the conscience of him which is weak be emboldened to eat those things which are offered to idols. (1 Corinthians 8:9-10.)

Why is it, in view of all the extra help and special grace we need, that God condescends to work through such individuals as ourselves? God's love! But, also, His determination to use the weak, foolish, and the despised of the world may have occurred because only such individuals are humble and pliable enough to perform His demanding chores. Perhaps God also desires to illustrate how He has the capacity to bring to pass His mighty and majestic purposes in the earth, even though He uses such individuals.

Perhaps, too, God's continuous demonstration of His divine power is needed so that we will learn to trust Him now in preparation for other tasks that are yet ahead of us, when we can be reminded of how He brought to pass His work on this planet, using the weak and the foolish and the despised.

The Lord has given stern reminders before. After the children of Israel had crossed over the "heaped up" and flooded Jordan River in a divine demonstration of power reminiscent of the Red Sea crossing, the Lord had them take twelve stones and place them in Gilgal as a reminder of that moment:

And those twelve stones, which they took out of Jordan, did Joshua pitch in Gilgal.

And he spake unto the children of Israel, saying, When your children shall ask their fathers in time to come, saying, What mean these stones?

Then ye shall let your children know, saying, Israel came over this Jordan on dry land.

For the Lord your God dried up the waters of Jordan from before you, until ye were passed over, as the Lord your God did to the Red sea, which he dried up from before us, until we were gone over:

That all the people of the earth might know the hand of the Lord, that it is mighty: that ye might fear the Lord your God for ever. (Joshua 4:20-24.)

Our journey is demanding enough that the need for reassurance as well as reminders is constant.

There is our need, too, since only One was perfect, for another form of reassurance—the reality of repentance and forgiveness: " . . . though your sins be as scarlet, they shall be as white as snow." (Isaiah 1:18.) We are further reassured by our generous Lord that if we repent and keep His commandments, our past sins will not even be *mentioned* to us. (Ezekiel 18:22.) Nor should we mention them to each other!

Thus we are to keep everlastingly at it, being nourished by these great promises, knowing that our journey is not the journey of one day but of a lifetime. Even so, the closer we come to the City of God, the more we will notice the remaining distance and our remaining weaknesses.

The prophet Nephi, who had progressed and advanced spiritually to a remarkable degree, still lamented about "sins which do so easily beset me." (2 Nephi 4:18.) Obviously, Nephi's sins were not major. But just as God cannot look upon sin with the least degree of allowance (D&C 1:31), *as we become more like Him, neither can we.* The best people have a heightened awareness of what little of the worst is still in them! Indeed, the divine discontent, the justifiable spiritual restlessness that we feel, is a natural follow-on feeling in the disciple who has taken the Lord's counsel to "make you a new heart and a new spirit." (Ezekiel 18:31.) The "new" in us is bound to notice the "old" that remains.

However, it is vital for us to realize that if we are keeping the commandments and doing our basic duties, we are to that extent succeeding in that thing. Our sincere striving and seeking to keep the commandments counts for more than we know. The Lord has said:

> Wherefore . . . seek ye earnestly the best gifts, always remembering for what they are given;
> For verily I say unto you, they are given for the benefit of those who love me and keep all my commandments, *and him that seeketh so to do*; that all may be benefited that seek or that ask of me, that ask and not for a sign that they may consume it upon their lusts. (D&C 46:8-9. Italics added.)

Life being thus lived *is* the process of working out our salvation. We are not waiting for something else to happen.

Yes, there will be additional challenges and further soul-stretching experiences, but what is happening in the "holy present" is "it." Insofar as we are proceeding, we are succeeding.

Moreover, Latter-day Saints need to remember that we who live now are being called upon to work out our salvation in a special time of intense and immense challenges—the last portion of the dispensation of the fulness of times during which great tribulation and temptation will occur, the elect will almost be deceived, and unrighteous people will be living much as they were in the days of Noah. It will be a time of polarization, as the Twelve foresaw in their declaration of 1845. Hardness of heart in many will produce other manifestations of hardness and coarseness. Civility will be one casualty of these conditions, and a lowered capacity to achieve reconciliation, whether in a marriage or between interest groups, will be another.

Therefore, though we have rightly applauded our ancestors for their spiritual achievements (and do not and must not discount them now), those of us who prevail today will have done no small thing. The special spirits who have been reserved to live in this time of challenges and who overcome will one day be praised for their stamina by those who pulled handcarts.

Those who were righteous in other ages, when the gospel light was snuffed out, will one day commend the current members of the Church who so live that the gospel light increased in its incandescence.

Those of ancient Israel who saw many signs and yet episodically relapsed will one day praise those in this dispensation who have believed "because of the word" *without* being compelled to be humble. (Alma 32:14.)

The Lamanites who were righteous in earlier times, especially, will praise their present posterity whose righteousness is bringing a blossoming of their seed.

Thus the contemporary righteous will earn the esteem of their admired predecessors. Finally, if we are faithful, even the righteous of the city of Enoch will fall upon our necks and kiss us, and we will mingle our tears with their tears! (Moses 7:63.)

Let us, therefore, notwithstanding our weaknesses, be reassured that the everyday keeping of the commandments and the doing of our duties is what it is all about. Customized and immediate reinforcement will come to us as we meet our challenges: "And secondly, he doth require that ye should do as he hath commanded you; for which if ye do, *he doth immediately bless you*; and therefore he hath paid you. And ye are still indebted unto him, and are, and will be, forever and ever; therefore, of what have ye to boast?" (Mosiah 2:24. Italics added.)

We are to keep the commandments all the time. We are, for instance, to pray regularly. We must all receive the necessary ordinances for ourselves and for our kindred dead. Happily, there are a number of duties that serve as reminders of the need to keep the basic commandments, duties that we must not dismiss merely because they seem beneath us. The keeping of journals, said President Kimball, is tied to the keeping of the fifth great commandment. Genealogical work is clearly interlaced with temple work, which, in turn, is tied to the vital ordinances necessary to our own basic salvation. The vows we have made are before us as we do work for our kindred dead.

In the midst of this interlacing, however, it is important for us to remember, to use just one example, that programs such as the Church's current recreation programs are aids and helps. These clearly provide needed fellowship, physical exercise, cultural development, opportunities for missionary work, and moments of needed recognition for individuals. However, Abraham and those about him apparently did not have an athletic program. We have it now and it is helpful.

In like manner, cultural and familial situations in other times were different. The number of righteous single individuals in other ages was not, as it is today, such that the Special Interests and like programs were needed. In more pastoral settings and times, there was not the need for Church aids such as student wards for members living in or near centers of learning.

Thus some programs and practices in the Church today are important aids but have not been constant necessities in every other age. Discerning disciples understand this.

There are important practices and administrative procedures in the Church today that may not have been performed in precisely parallel ways in the Church in past dispensations. However, practices and methods may vary from age to age, but the commandments are constant. President Harold B. Lee told us to "keep in mind that the principles of the gospel of Jesus Christ are divine. Nobody changes the principles and doctrines of the Church except the Lord by revelation. But methods change as the inspired direction comes to those who preside at a given time." ("God's Kingdom—A Kingdom of Order," *Ensign*, January 1971, p.10.)

Thus the "methods" (the programs and the aids that the Lord uses to assist us) are very important. *They are means, however, and not ends in themselves.*

Moving forward is what the Lord expects of us. The Lord has even given us needed aids. He has placed markers along the way to guide us and milestones to pace us. After all, we are not engaged in the equivalent of the dashing flight of the bumblebee; ours is a very different journey.

God has told us that life itself passes away "as it were unto us a dream." (Jacob 7:26.) Into the brief, fleeting time allotted to each of us must be crowded challenges that will help us, in our weaknesses, to develop the qualities we now lack. The presence of stress may be needed for their development. Otherwise, the adversary could taunt us as he did Job by saying that an insulated Job was an untested Job. (See Job 1:8-12.) The same availability to experience adversity will be ours, for "the Lord seeth fit to chasten his people; yea, he trieth their patience and their faith." (Mosiah 23:21.) To expect immunity is naiveté!

In overcoming our weaknesses, pain is almost inevitable—perhaps even some exposure and embarrassment. We who live now should not expect to read comfortably in the scriptures about how predecessor disciples were visibly reproved "on the record" and blithely assume that there will be no more such visible examples. We ourselves may become such!

Motivation *can* arise out of humiliation, just as determination *can* grow out of deprivation. Opportunity may lie hidden within seeming tragedy. Conscientious Christians who are conscious of their own weaknesses—but not immobilized by them—understand this.

When soul-stretched, our later declarations of love of God and of our trust in Him will carry a special authenticity, as did this testimony from Alma: "And I have been supported under trials and troubles of every kind, yea, and in all manner of afflictions; yea, God has delivered me from prison, and from bonds, and from death; yea, and I do put my trust in him, and he will still deliver me." (Alma 36:27.)

The exemplar's eloquence may go unheeded by some, but it cannot be surpassed in its authenticity. The authority of character that, unlike pudding, is not whipped up in an instant, and earned esteem are powerful, as this episode in the life of George Washington illustrates:

Washington called together the grumbling officers on March 15, 1783. They filled the hall called the Temple, which served for worship, dances, and conferences. He began to speak—carefully and from a written manuscript, referring to the proposal of "either deserting our Country in the extremist hour of her distress, or turning our Arms against it. . . . " Washington appealed simply and honestly for reason, restraint, patience, and duty—all the good and unexciting virtues.

And then Washington stumbled as he read. He squinted, paused, and out of his pocket he drew some new spectacles.

"Gentlemen, you must pardon me," he said in apology. "I have grown gray in your service and now find myself growing blind."

Most of his men had never seen the general wear glasses. Yes, the men said to themselves, eight hard years. They recalled the ruddy, full-blooded planter of 1775; now they saw . . . a big, good, fatherly man grown old. They wept, many of those warriors. And the Newburgh plot dissolved. (Bart McDowell, *Revolutionary War*, The National Geographic Society, 1967, pp. 190-91.)

If we are righteous and faithful, we will come to see, as did Joseph of Eqypt, that character is often developed in the cauldron of trial, for the seeming tragedy of his youth contained within it opportunities (which did not fully appear for many years) to "save much people alive." (Genesis 50:20.) "Much" probably was millions who were fed by Joseph's national food storage plan. The evil intent of Joseph's brothers was folded into the plans of God, who knows the beginning from the end and all that is in between.

We do not, of course, rejoice in our weaknesses, for while God uses us notwithstanding our weaknesses, it is because certain weaknesses can humble us and render us more susceptible to His shaping, which shaping will, one day, patiently knead these weaknesses out of us. We must not, however, come to enjoy our weaknesses!

Only an omniscient and omniloving God could use the weak and foolish. And because His love for us is perfect, as is His knowledge of our personal possibilities, there is no real question of His accepting us. But He does so without being content with what we now are. Our self-acceptance must strike the same balance.

Hence we must be serious about this joy-filled trek notwithstanding our inadequacies. God supplies the commandments, the ordinances, the opportunities, and the aids. We must make the choices, perform the duties, and, in a brisk pace, walk in His ways, especially remembering to keep His two basic commandments on which everything else hangs.

# 2

## *On These Two Hang*
## *All the Law and the Prophets*

The Savior made a stunning declaration when He said that *all* the law and prophets hang on the first and second commandments. (Matthew 22:40.) Who could compress all the commandments into but two or scale their significance better than their Author? And who needs this perspective more than the disciple who strives to move forward notwithstanding his weaknesses?

When these two rigorous requirements receive more deep reflection than is usually given to them, one observes that there is a significant difference in the breathtaking wording of the first great commandment compared with that of the second commandment. We are to love God with *all* our *heart, all* our *mind, all* our *soul,* and *all* our *strength*. But we are to love our neighbors as we love ourselves. (Matthew 22:36-40; Mark 12:29-34; Luke 10:25-28.)

The first commandment does *not* read, "Thou shalt love the Lord thy God as thyself." This would be both too little and the wrong kind of love. Nor does the second commandment read, "Thou shalt love they neighbor with all thy heart, mind, soul, and strength." This would be neighbor worship.

Whereas our Perfect Father can be trusted with our

bestowal of all our devotion of heart, mind, soul, and strength, we cannot. Nor can our neighbor. Moreover, only when proper love of God comes *first* can our love of self and neighbor be safely shaped and nurtured.

Colonial clergyman Jonathan Edwards said, in effect, "What was wrong with believers and unbelievers in general . . . was that they had little ideas about a little God." True religion brings us to "a loving of God rather than a believing that one ought to love Him, active concern for the neighbor rather than acceptance of this statement that love of neighbor is very good," which makes all the difference in the world. (*Christian Ethics*, New York: Ronald Press, 1955, pp. 383, 385.)

The personality of God involves the balanced perfection of His attributes, which makes Him worthy of worship and adoration. God can safely have absolute power because He also has absolute love and because He is perfect in His judgment. He can give His perfect mercy full play because He is also perfect in His justice. But no such perfection or balance exists either in us or in our neighbors. Thus the extension of our genuine esteem to our neighbors is different in kind and not just degree from that total love we are told to develop for God.

We could, of course, never truly keep the first commandment without also keeping the second commandment. But the second commandment flows from the first commandment, and all the other commandments are steppingstones running from the two great commandments.

Besides, how can one really love and serve his neighbor if he ignores the divinely designed purpose of the universe? How can we fully serve our neighbor if we do not acknowledge who our neighbor really is? In a day when the ecological needs of the snail darter are carefully considered, do we really suppose we can truly serve others if we ignore the everlasting ecology of which they are a part?

Thus our relationship with God is clearly the central relationship on which all other relationships hang. This reality is especially important in today's world wherein many either ignore the Fatherhood of God altogether or subordinate it to a simulated and secular brotherhood of man—and thus fail at both relationships.

In our foolishness and weakness, it is the beginning of both wisdom and strength to understand the obligations and the implications of the first commandment, though, as we come closer to Him, our weaknesses come to light, sometimes painfully. To remain in darkness is to fail to know Him and ourselves! Can there be a more serious and disabling deprivation? Of our life in His universe, as George MacDonald counseled, "The instant a soul moves counter to the will of its prime mover, the universe is its prison." (*Life Essential*, Wheaton, Ill.: Harold Shaw Publishers, 1974, p. 100.)

To put God in any place other than first is to put down our own eternal interests. There can be demonstrated in our lives (and in so many other ways) the terrible tyranny of secondary and thirdly things.

It is not just the tyranny of trivia—that problem is vexing but manageable. It is, rather, the chronic pattern in which we misread our primary purposes on this planet, misspend our precious time, misappropriate our needed talents and means—behaving so parochially in the face of the great galactic realities of "things as they really are." (Jacob 4:13.) It is this constant inversion that demeans us, diminishes our joy, and locks us into being far less than we might become. Even when we repent, we still cannot recycle the time lost nor do retroactively the good deeds that might have been.

Such consequences stem from our basic failure to put first things first, specifically our relationship with God. Only when that relationship is in order do we see other things clearly. Until then, like the patient belatedly being tested for eyeglasses, we do not even realize what we have been missing. So it is when we begin to see with the eye of faith.

Perhaps the singular reference to the *eye* of faith, rather than *eyes* of faith, is to stress that our eye should be *single* to the glory of God—"one eye, . . . one faith, and one baptism," which brings unity and love. (Mosiah 18:21.) Jesus taught that "the light of the body is the eye," and that if our eye is single we will be "full of light." (3 Nephi 13:22.) As with the natural eye, the eye of faith lets in the light of the Lord; we do not make light ourselves but, rather, use His! Those who so live, once inside the veil, will truly see "with their eyes the things which they had beheld with an eye of faith, and they were glad." (Ether 12:19.) Thus our present view of things—whether dark and dim or bright and full—fashions, irrevocably, our future. And our view of things turns on our views of Christ and of our Heavenly Father. (Alma 27:28.)

In a world in which more and more people ignore the first commandment and live "without God in the world," we see in those lives a fatal separation from reality. First of all, to live "without God in the world" is, said Alma, a condition "contrary to the nature of happiness." (Alma 41:11.) Having gone wrong as to the first commandment, everything else is then askew, including relationships with others. As for such souls, their mortal lives are "no more than a night in a second-class hotel." (Saint Teresa of Avila.)

A secularized second commandment is no substitute for the real thing. It was Dostoevsky who warned (in a grim foreshadowing of the secular state) that "love toward men . . . without belief in God, very naturally leads to the greatest coercion over men and turns their lives completely into hell on earth." Those who rule and govern without any real allegiance to God may use the rhetoric of serving "the people," but they will end up doing wrong things for and to "the people." Whether because of ignorance or malice, such individuals will misread mankind's identity or purpose, and this misreading inevitably means misery. Furthermore, as Brigham Young observed, "Man's machinery makes things alike" (JD 9:370), while God gives to seemingly like individuals pleasing differences. Secularism is no friend of righteous individuality.

Still others concede that both the first and second commandments are central but say these are so unreachable; therefore, why strive to distinguish between them? Yet Jesus called upon us to be "perfect even as your Father which is in heaven is perfect." (Matthew 5:48.) Would a Lord who cannot lie taunt us with any possibility that is irrevocably out of our reach? With God's helping grace, Moroni promised, we can become "holy, without spot." (Moroni 10:33.)

It can be done, but not all at once—just as Enoch's great city and its people reached a pinnacle of progress only "in process of time." Then they were taken to the bosom of God. (Moses 7.)

As we grow "in process of time," neighbors will suffer less and less at our hands. Then one will naturally esteem his neighbor as himself, because he understands who his neighbor really is. Each step toward singlemindedness in our worship of God squeezes out some of our selfishness, for so much of the overcoming of this world consists of overcoming selfishness. After all, which neighbor fares better—the one who lives by him who is filled with love, patience, and hope, or the one who lives by him who is self-ish, impatient, and despairing?

With increasing charity, then, our service to others will be an unforced thing—it will be a thing from inside, not from outside! Even the good we then do will be done for the right reasons and "not to please ourselves." (Romans 15:1.)

When we truly love God, we are released from the cruel constraints of our own egos. As our capacity to love in-creases, we go beyond the giving of time and talents and means—on to the full giving of self. Presently, so many of us send checks where we are not willing to go. So many of us give our time, but our hearts and minds are elsewhere.

Progress in relation to the first commandment will also bring us ever closer to having the "mind of Christ" with no disposition to bear false witness against another and no de-sire to defraud. (See 2 Corinthians 2:16.)

As we learn so to love, we will become more lovable, making much less taxing the task others have of loving us. Our neighbors will be better treated as we become better, for righteousness is more self-reinforcing than evil is.

One will neither covet what a neighbor has nor shrink from truthfully warning a neighbor. The same tough love one applies to himself will not, condescendingly, be with-held from a neighbor who may need us to *level* with him be-fore he can be *lifted* up.

Even enemies are prayed for, since, ultimately, there are no enemies among our brothers and sisters. True, some friendships have yet to be formed; some deep differences have yet to be dissolved; some tongues still bear false witness—but those same tongues will one day openly confess that Jesus is the Christ, with all that acknowledgment implies. (See Romans 14:10-12; Mosiah 28:31.)

God is anxious to take us as far as we who are weak are willing to go in this journey toward perfection. It will not be He who disappoints. He knows our possibilities and will not settle for less, though, alas, we may. He knows what we need, while we merely know what we want.

Meanwhile, it is so easy to skim across the surface of those words which tell us about one of the outcomes of keeping the first and second commandments in this journey of discovery: "He that loseth his life for my sake shall find it." (Matthew 10:39.) One can likewise merely regard the Sermon on the Mount as being "nice"—without being stunned by the deep demands it makes of us, in furtherance of the first commandment. This is especially so in our age when "the love of many will wax cold" and when people are "lovers of their own selves." (Matthew 24:12; 2 Timothy 3:2.)

But to keep the first commandment, we must lose our lives *for His sake,* and the gospel's—not just for any cause. (Mark 8:35.) The Lord, in modern revelation, restated and then amplified the first commandment by adding these eleven words about the very particularized way in which we are to love God: "And in the name of Jesus Christ thou shalt serve him." (D&C 59:5.)

We simply cannot develop the love of God demanded by the first commandment if our hearts are elsewhere! True, we can spend our lives sincerely, as so many do, in other useful endeavors, but, comparatively, these are low-yield endeavors.

Jesus' entreaty—"Come follow me"—reminds us that losing our life for His sake is to enter into a directed thing. It is a tutorial trek, not the wandering of each individual walking stubbornly in his own way.

When we are busy serving Him, there is no time to think much of self and, of course, that is part of the training. Just as those who are learning to dance are not really dancing if they have to think about each next step, so the righteous life eventually becomes partly a matter of reflex.

But keeping the first commandment is an act of high trust; we turn ourselves over to our Father and finally give Him all that we have. Happily, He has said that, one day, we can enter His presence and receive *all* that He has. But we simply cannot contain all that He has to give until we are first emptied and then expanded. Until then, we are only part-time and seasonal workers in His vineyard.

Only when our commitment is full can we be fully used by Him. The more we are centered on Him the less we are centered on self. The relentlessly self-centered find the second commandment to be too distracting and too demanding because such are self-pleasers and are envious. Keepers of the first commandment are innocent of envy. Besides, only when our motives are good can our performance be consecrated for our good. (See 2 Nephi 32:9.)

Some say that the leap of faith is when we begin to believe in God, and that is, indeed, a very significant moment. However, the real leap occurs when the beginning believer forsakes his self-centeredness and begins loving God with all his heart, mind, soul, and strength. Compliance with that first commandment takes us on a journey that is so demanding that many never even try it. It is a journey that requires a complete letting go of the old self and old ways. No wonder God has declared that all the law and the prophets hang on the first and second commandments!

Such love of the Lord requires that we become trusting-
ly patient as experiences come to us that God deems are for
our good. We must, on this side of the veil, wait out the in-
explicable things, maintaining serenity as the storms beat
upon us and as the winds of derision howl. We must be
willing to submit ourselves "to all things which the Lord
seeth fit to inflict" upon us. (Mosiah 3:19.) This is the unconditional submittal of the soul that lies at the very center
of the first great commandment; there can be no holding
back. Only as we thus come close to the living Lord can
we honestly say, in the midst of the fiery trials of life, "Not
as I will, but as thou wilt." (Matthew 26:39.)

Such righteous performance brings a closeness to Him
and enables us to reach breaking points without breaking.

Such love requires that we go on serving—even when
some say it is senseless and useless to help others and as
still others try to depersonalize human relationships or to
bureaucratize all brotherhood. It causes rejoicing over his
gift of life to us when others say that life is without mean-
ing. It asks us to be fully submissive to God in a world in
which selfishness parades about as individualism, an apostate individualism.

Such total love of and obedience to God means also that
we no longer presume to teach God knowledge or murmur
at the manner in which His plans unfold. If we are driven to
ask why, it is an interrogatory that springs from our knowing that He *is* there and that there *is* an answer—even
though we do not yet know the answer! Otherwise, we
would not even put the question.

As we come to understand and experience God in all of
His perfected attributes and as we struggle to develop
these same attributes in ourselves, we move from appreciation for Him to adoration of Him.

Just as the love of God for us is unconditional, one day ours for Him must be likewise. This is what the first commandment is all about. But even then, the adoration and awe we have developed for God will take humble notice of the eternal fact, stressed by John, that God loved us first. (See 1 John 4:19.) As we come closer to Him, we not only "stand all amazed"—we even kneel all amazed!

Thus, far from feeling that the commandments—especially the first two—"cramp our style," we ought to realize, as the writer of Proverbs wisely said, "The commandment is a lamp" (Proverbs 6:23); it is a necessity to light our journey along the straight and narrow way in a darkening world. Likewise, as the writer of Ecclesiastes said, the keeping of the commandments is "the whole duty of man." (Ecclesiastes 12:13.) We do not have any other duties worth mentioning in the same breath.

Thus the keeping of the commandments opens up and illuminates life. Obedience does not diminish us, as in righteousness we learn more, we feel more, we see more. It is sensuality and sin that close us in and take us to a point where we are "past feeling." (See 1 Nephi 17:45; Ephesians 4:19; Moroni 9:20.)

Though the world sees it differently, righteous obeying is growing; righteous complying is stretching. President Marion G. Romney has said, for instance, that one of the ways he can tell when he is speaking under the inspiration of heaven is that he actually learns from what he says. Job made a somewhat parallel observation: " . . . therefore have I uttered that I understood not; things too wonderful for me, which I knew not." (Job 42:3.)

In a very real way, therefore, disobedience to the first commandment (denying Jesus Christ, who literally "bought" us and ransomed us) is to deny our own development. Such denial has far graver consequences than is realized by those who think the first commandment is a mere theological or liturgical nicety.

The neglect of the first two commandments is felt more than in the soul of the individual who ceases to believe; the awful results spread till they touch all of society.

Efforts to move away from our traditional values, such as belief in God, produce terrible paradoxes. Decrease the belief in God, for instance, and you increase the numbers of those who wish to play at being God. Such societal supervisors deny the existence of divine standards but are very serious about imposing their own—or the lack of them.

It is no accident that the lessening, or loss, of belief in certain absolute truths, such as the existence of God and the reality of immortality, has occurred at the same time there has been a sharp gain in the size and power of governments.

Once we remove belief in God from the center of our lives, as the source of truth and as a determiner of justice, a tremendous vacuum is created into which selfishness surges, a condition that governments delight in managing.

Tens of thousands of regulations emerging from governments receive attention not given the Ten Commandments, perhaps because the Ten Commandments, which are so much a part of our Judeo-Christian heritage, are not flexible; they resist rationalization. Any amendments to the Ten Commandments could come only from the original Source. We cannot amend the seventh commandment to read, for instance, "Thou shalt not commit adultery except between consenting adults."

We are, of course, free to obey or not to obey those commandments discarding the lamp noted in Proverbs. But we cannot get that lamp to make light by using a substitute fuel. We may, by legislation and regulation, vainly try to create a zone of private morality. But there is, ultimately, no such thing as private morality; there are not an indoor set and an outdoor set of Ten Commandments.

Those who disavow the existence of certain absolute truths must forever forgo disapproving of anything on moral grounds. They may try to evoke a social or political response by using the old words that went with the old values, but they will soon learn that words cannot, for long, be appropriated productively minus their moral content.

There remains only one way to get outside the small cell of self-interest: we must first love God and in the name of Jesus Christ serve Him, proceeding onward to the loving and esteeming of our fellowmen even as, when enlightened, we regard ourselves.

Our very happiness is at stake, and keeping the commandments is the key. Jonathan Edwards said that "happiness is the end of creation." How parallel to the utterance of the Prophet Joseph Smith, who said: "Happiness is the object and design of our existence; and will be the end thereof, if we pursue the path that leads to it; and this path is virtue, uprightness, faithfulness, holiness, and keeping all the commandments of God." (*Teachings of the Prophet Joseph Smith*, pp. 255-56.)

How like, too, the observation in the Book of Mormon that "men are, that they might have joy." (2 Nephi 2:25.)

Thus the keeping of the first great commandment is fundamental to everything. Indeed, to live without God in the world *is* contrary to the nature of happiness!

Far from being some mysterious, inscrutable "life force" off in space that dabbles in human affairs occasionally, the living God is lovingly assertive. For instance, in the not-distant future, those who live without God in the world and who deny the Lord who bought them will experience His directiveness very dramatically; when Jesus Christ appears again and "all flesh" shall see Him together, "all nations shall tremble" at his presence. (See 2 Peter 2:1; D&C 101:23; D&C 133:42.) Jesus will then begin His reign "over all flesh" (D&C 133:25); there will be "a full end of all nations" (D&C 87:6), and "no laws but my laws when I come" (D&C 38:22). When the Lord of the vineyard returns, it will be the "natives" who undergo a cosmic cultural shock!

The Savior's second coming will thus swiftly silence the needless debate carried on by some over the so-called historicity of Jesus Christ. Those who viewed Him only as a "little god" and as a "moral teacher," having hope in Christ only in this life, will in that awful moment be "of all men most miserable." (1 Corinthians 15:19.)

But we must make no mistake about it. The deceptions of the world will be clever and the pull of the world real and insistent. Life in the last days will be filled with tribulation and temptation and deception and polarization—so much so that if it were possible, the very elect would be deceived. (Matthew 24:24-26.) In such darkness, so much greater is the need for God's laws and for the light of the gospel, for "the commandment is a lamp; and the law is light." (Proverbs 6:23.) Those of us seeking to progress, notwithstanding our weaknesses, dare not try to go forward lampless!

While the polarization is underway and will produce some special pressures and strains on the members of the Church, we must not be dismayed by it. In some ways, we ought to be grateful. The alternatives facing the children of men will be sharpened; the decisions required will be more clear-cut, the time in which to decide shortened.

Thus, as the Church comes forth out of obscurity, as its

light can no longer be hidden, and as the Lord bares His arm and the events foreseen by Him begin to roll forth in the final days, those whose concerns for the Church consist mostly of wishing to be well liked will have a hard time. There is no way that the Church and its prophets can help the bad people of the world to feel good. There is no way that the gospel's behavioral standards can be fudged. Natural as our desire for rapport, friendship, and affection is, we must be more concerned with "being alienated from the life of God." (Ephesians 4:18.) Being accepted by God is more important than being accepted by the world, as these eloquent words of Malcolm Muggeridge witness:

> When I look back on my life nowadays, which I sometimes do, what strikes me most forcibly about it is that what seemed at the time most significant and seductive, seems now most futile and absurd. For instance, success in all of its various guises; being known and being praised; ostensible pleasures, like acquiring money or seducing women, or traveling, going to and fro in the world and up and down in it like Satan, exploring and experiencing whatever Vanity Fair has to offer.
>
> In retrospect all these exercises in self-gratification seem pure fantasy, what Pascal called "licking the earth." They are diversions designed to distract our attention from the true purpose of our existence in this world, which is, quite simply, to look for God, and, in looking, to find Him, and, having found Him, to love Him, thereby establishing a harmonious relationship with His purposes for His creation. (*A Twentieth Century Testimony*, Thomas Nelson Inc., 1978.)

The sooner we renounce the world, the better we are able to help the world! Unlike experiencing in "Vanity Fair," experiencing a belief in and a true love of the true and living God will produce the result the prophet Ether described, filling believers with a sure "hope for a better world, yea, even a place at the right hand of God, which hope cometh of faith, maketh an anchor to the souls of men, which would make them sure and steadfast, always abounding in good works, being led to glorify God." (Ether 12:4.)

In contrast, unbelief produces a situation in which people are "led about by Satan, even as chaff is driven before the wind, or as a vessel is tossed about upon the waves, without sail or anchor, or without anything wherewith to steer her; and even as she is, so are they." (Mormon 5:18.)

This is what happens, said Mormon, when people do not have "Christ for their shepherd." (V. 17.) No matter when or where we start this journey, it is a journey to be made notwithstanding our weaknesses, but with Him as our Shepherd. Jesus said, "And whosoever doth not bear his cross, and come after me, cannot be my disciple." (Luke 14:27).

Significantly, in the Joseph Smith Translation of that same verse, these sobering words were added, which reflect the deep demands of the first commandment: "Wherefore, *settle this in your hearts*, that ye will do the things which I shall teach, and command you." (JST, Luke 14:28. Italics added). To love God and obey Him is a decision that must be firmly *settled in our hearts*. Ambivalence is a hindrance, and indecision is a decision.

Even having so chosen God, however, we cannot expect immunity from anxiety or challenge. On one occasion, Paul described his weariness and feelings with considerable candor: "For, when we were come into Macedonia, our flesh had no rest, but we were troubled on every side; without were fightings, within were fears." (2 Corinthians 7:5.)

Therefore, notwithstanding our weaknesses, our task is to improve the world in God's way rather than to be merely "conformed to this world." We are to be transformed (Romans 12:2) and to be transformers, including in such unusual circumstances as those that will finally shake even the kingdom of the devil in order that those "which belong to it must needs be stirred up unto repentance." (2 Nephi 28:19.)

Could we have been asked to keep the two great commandments in a more adventure-filled time?

However, before we leave the discussion of the first two commandments, it is not amiss to declare again how all of God's commandments matter and are so interrelated—including even the tenth commandment pertaining to coveting. The late and wise Elder Richard L. Evans wrote: "It all adds up to this: None of the commandments stand alone. The breaking of any one of them weakens the will to keep all the others: And the commandments against coveting cannot be lightly looked upon—nor can any other commandment." (*The Ten Commandments Today*, Deseret Book, 1955, p.145.)

How could it be otherwise, for since the commandments are like lamps, is it not obedience to them that gives to us the illumination necessary for a "perfect brightness of hope"?

# 3

## *A Perfect Brightness of Hope*

Hope—of the right kind—is an essential trait and quality for the disciples who proceed forward on the "straight and narrow path" notwithstanding their weaknesses.

When we speak of hope as a Christian virtue, however, it is necessary to disengage ourselves from the world's notions of hope. The latter are, at best, rather vague and are often tied to ephemeral enthusiasm, such as Richard Cobden's 1846 speech in England celebrating the "most important event in history" since the coming of Christ—"the repeal of the corn laws." Human hyperbole is an unreliable source of perspective.

Worldly hope is not always focused on justified objects. Hence it is that some disbelievers who discern the vagueness of worldly hope scorn it and therefore, wrongly, see all hope as naive and as lacking realistic supporting evidence.

Real hope, said Paul, is a hope for things that are not seen that are true. (See Romans 8:24.) Paul accurately linked hopelessness and godlessness as he wrote of those "having no hope, and without God in the world." (Ephesians 2:12.) Christ-centered hope, however, is a very specific and particularized hope. It is focused on the great reali-

40

ties of the resurrection, eternal life, a better world, and Christ's triumphant second coming—"things as they really *will be*." (Jacob 4:13. Italics added.)

Moroni asked rhetorically, "What should we hope for?" and, responding, said: "Behold I say unto you that ye shall have hope through the atonement of Christ and the power of his resurrection, to be raised unto life eternal, and this because of your faith in him according to the promise." (Moroni 7:41.)

Paul described the resurrection-orientation of our hope with equal explicitness: "But I would not have you to be ignorant, brethren, concerning them which are asleep, that ye sorrow not, even as others which have no hope. For if we believe that Jesus died and rose again, even so them also which sleep in Jesus will God bring with him." (1 Thessalonians 4:13-14.)

Moroni attested that if we believe in God, we can with "surety hope for a better world, . . . which hope cometh of faith, making an anchor to the souls of man, which would make them sure and steadfast, always abounding in good works." (Ether 12:4.) Paul earlier analogized hope as an "anchor to the soul." (Hebrews 6:19.)

Thus gospel hope is a very focused and particularized hope that is based upon justified expectations. It is a virtue that is intertwined with faith and charity, which virtues are not to be understood either when they are torn apart from each other *or apart from the Lord Jesus Christ*, without whom they are all vague virtues. Doubt and despair go together, whereas faith and hope are constant companions. Those, for instance, who "hope" in vain for (and speak of) the day of world peace when men "shall beat their swords into plowshares" ignore the reality that the millennial dawn will be ushered in only by the second coming of Jesus

Christ. Neither secular rhetoric nor secular assemblies will succeed in bringing lasting peace to this planet. Secularists, meanwhile, have ironically appropriated the Lord's language of hope while denying Him! It is He and His ways alone that can bring about such desirable conditions. There will be no millennium without the Master.

Paul's futuring focused on the Lord, giving us consolation by holding forth that which is to come, confirming hope. But this hope develops, as does faith, "line upon line, precept upon precept; here a little, and there a little." (D&C 128:21.)

It is to be understood, however, that hope is not the same as perfect knowledge. (See Alma 32:21.) Once we have actually seen, said Paul, it "is not hope." (Romans 8:24.) Thus hope, like faith, is not quite knowledge. Yet, being at the border of knowledge, we can see through "glass darkly" enough of the future to affect how we live today.

Indeed, one of the virtues necessary for us to remain on the straight and narrow path, said Nephi, is a "perfect brightness of hope." (2 Nephi 31:20.) "Brightness" connotes a vividness and a preciseness just as does "a bright recollection of our guilt" (Alma 11:43), which would involve a vivid and precise recollection. Worldly hope is dull or vague, not what we read of in the scriptures about "a more excellent hope": "And I also remember that thou hast said that thou hast prepared a house for man, yea, even among the mansions of thy Father in which man might have *a more excellent hope*: wherefore man must hope or he cannot receive an inheritance in the place which thou hast prepared." (Ether 12:32. Italics added.)

Christian hope draws upon reliable witnesses from the past and is based on accumulative experience: "Wherefore, we search the prophets, and we have many revelations and the spirit of prophecy; *and having all these witnesses we obtain a hope,* and our faith becometh unshaken, insomuch that we truly can command in the name of Jesus and the very trees obey us, or the mountains, or the waves of the sea." (Jacob 4:6. Italics added.)

These glorious words of hope are based on glorious encounters: "And again, the voice of God in the chamber of old Father Whitmer, in Fayette, Seneca county, and at sundry times, and in divers places through all the travels and tribulations of this Church of Jesus Christ of Latter-day Saints! And the voice of Michael, the archangel; the voice of Gabriel, and of Raphael, and of divers angels, from Michael or Adam down to the present time, all declaring their dispensation, their rights, their keys, their honors, their majesty and glory, and the power of their priesthood; giving line upon line, precept upon precept; here a little, and there a little; giving us consolation by holding forth that which is to come, *confirming our hope!*" (D&C 128:21. Italics added.)

Even our righteous experience brings hope: "And not only so, but we glory in tribulations also: knowing that tribulation worketh patience; And patience, experience; and experience, hope." (Romans 5:3-4.)

Quite clearly, therefore, ultimate hope is tied to the verifiable expectation of a resurrection and the better world to follow. Paul observed that if our hope in Christ pertained to "this life only," a resurrectionless view of Christ, we would be "of all men most miserable." (1 Corinthians 15:19.) In other words, proximate hope, disengaged from the reality of the resurrection (what some inconsistently espouse as a Christian existentialism), is not Christian hope at all! As Edward Norman observed:

At the centre of the Christian religion, Christ remains unchanging in a world of perpetual social change and mutating values. To identify him with the passing enthusiasms of men—each one of which, in its time of acceptance, seems permanently true—is to lose him amidst the shifting superstructure of human idealism.

Christians are those who act under the permanent rule that the ways of God are not the ways of men. They will cooperate with others to promote the eradication of agreed injustices, but they will, unlike them, recognize that their language of principles, and the cultural materials in which they are expressed, are wholly unstable. They will act, therefore, as individuals, not merely in charitable palliatives but in corporate and political action, according to their understanding. . . . There can be no proper identification of Christianity with human idealism. Cooperation with the world is always on the world's own terms. (*Christianity and the World Order*, pp. 77, 79.)

When we have appropriate hope of receiving eternal life (Alma 13:29), and we retain that hope through faith (Alma 25:16), then we will—even though we love life, family, and friends—have "no terror of death" "because of [our] hope and views of Christ and the resurrection." (Alma 27:28.) Indeed, true hope springs directly from our "views of Christ."

No wonder the writer of Proverbs could say that "the hope of the righteous is gladness." (Proverbs 10:28.) Because of the attitudinal anchor that gospel hope gives us in life, it is vital (in terms of avoiding being tossed to and fro) just as is membership in His prophet-led Church, which also keeps us from being tossed to and fro by every manner of doctrine. (See Ephesians 4:11-14.)

Our hope is such a great blessing, as Paul so graphically recorded, for it rescues us from anomie and alienation: "That at that time ye were without Christ, being aliens from the commonwealth of Israel, and strangers from the covenants of promise, *having no hope*, and *without God* in the world." (Ephesians 2:12. Italics added.)

And how precious—as we contemplate this sobering

and yet promising verse—is our hope compared to the stress that lies ahead for those whose lives continue to be lived "without God in the world": "Yea, every knee shall bow, and every tongue confess before him. Yea, even at the last day, when all men shall stand to be judged of him, then shall they confess that he is God; then shall they confess, who live *without God in the world,* that the judgment of an everlasting punishment is just upon them; and they shall quake, and tremble, and shrink beneath the glance of his all-searching eye." (Mosiah 27:31. Italics added.)

However, our hope, unless it is strong, can be at the mercy of our moods and can be badgered and bullied by events and by the contempt of the world, which we will experience in rather large doses in the irreligious last part of the last dispensation. Part of the contempt of the world comes because the worldly do not understand the things of the Spirit and regard such as foolishness and stupidity. Therefore, attacks on the Church are not always rebuttable *in worldly terms.* There are those who are multilingual but cannot communicate in the mother tongue of faith. Sometimes the best response is a certain silence, such as that of the Master before Pilate.

The adversary has done well in persuading many people that those who are religious are naive, ineffectual, or insincere Elmer Gantry types along with promoting the deception that any authoritarian religious commitment automatically means a Jonestown. Furthermore, these usual stereotypes about those who stoutly refuse to "be conformed unto this world" permit disbelievers to be patronizing toward the religious by suggesting that such individuals are congenitally incapable of making any real civic, political, social, or educational contributions. In reality, of course, those who are deeply persuaded and consistently performing Christians not only bring salvation to their own souls but also provide a much-needed balance for the many who are so entangled in the webbing of the world.

Ironically, the true believer in Christ—because of his keeping (to a high degree) the two great commandments—is tolerant of those who feel and believe otherwise; however, some secularists are increasingly intolerant, tending to dismiss the views of those with religious convictions as if these views are of no account, since they issue from those who are, somehow, second-class citizens.

One would be appalled to hear anyone dismiss the views of a black person concerning civil rights by saying simply, "Oh, you're just saying that because you're black!" It seems quite appropriate to some, however, to dismiss those who oppose abortion by saying, "Oh, you're just saying that because you're a Catholic."

Religious values and experience are bound to shape one's views concerning the issues of the day, a reality for which there need be no apology. Others may freely choose not to attach weight to those views, but to dismiss them out of hand is hardly the characteristic that ought to prevail in a true democracy.

Without this special hope, it is difficult for the gospel to work in us in order to bring about the changes and the needed improvements in ourselves and in society. President Joseph F. Smith warned that the gospel causes disturbances, for "we get in the way of purely human affairs and disturb the current of life in many ways and in many places. People who are comfortably located and well provided for do not like to be disturbed. . . . We have our particular mission to perform; and that we may perform it in consonance with divine purposes, we are running counter to the ways of man. We are made unpopular. The contempt of the world is on us, and we are the unloved child among the peoples of the earth." (*Gospel Doctrine*, pp. 118-19.)

But those who have gospel hope are willing to endure their often misunderstood as well as misrepresented role in the world and, at the same time, to let their hope work within them. Hope is both a developmental virtue and a virtue to be developed. Therefore, we should not be surprised if it involves some pain, especially in the difficult circumstances noted above.

The Prophet Joseph Smith was struck by the important and often ignored fact that John made such a point that hope also helps us to purify ourselves: "Beloved, now are we the sons of God, and it doth not yet appear what we shall be: but we know that, when he shall appear, we shall be like him; for we shall see him as he is. And every man that hath *this hope* in him *purifieth* himself, even as he is pure." (1 John 3:2-3. Italics added.)

The Prophet Joseph stressed the importance of our receiving a "crown of righteousness" and how hope—precise, gospel hope—can help us to purify ourselves! (*Teachings of the Prophet Joseph Smith*, p. 64.)

Thus we see, again and again, that just as the faith spoken of is a particularized faith—faith in the resurrected Lord Jesus Christ—so the hope spoken of is a particularized hope, a hope for a glorious resurrection and all that the atonement of Christ promises us.

Unsurprisingly, the charity spoken of in the triad of "faith, hope, and charity" is, likewise, a particularized charity—it is the pure love of Christ! (Moroni 7:47.) The pure love of Christ obviously means that the central objects of our love are our Heavenly Father and Jesus Christ—in effect, keeping the first great commandment. But the pure love of Christ also speaks to the need to develop the quality of our love till it becomes like the pure love Christ has for us. Then can we be called the "peaceable followers of Christ." (Moroni 7:3-4.) Such individuals, filled with love, can walk among the children of men carrying these marvelous, absolute truths with them, being enunciatory and yet contributory, and nurturing the necessary relationships with others.

Of course, faith, hope, and charity are not exclusive, but are mutual and interacting gifts. Since, for instance, despair cometh because of iniquity, then true hope cometh because of righteousness. Righteousness reinforces in us these three sterling attributes spoken of so often in the scriptures.

Without faith, hope, and charity the Lord has pointedly said that we "can do nothing" (D&C 18:19)—nothing that really matters everlastingly. Furthermore, just as faith precedes the kind of hope being spoken of, we can have neither of these, the prophets tell us, if we are not (even before then) "meek, and lowly of heart." (Moroni 7:43.) It is this same meekness that makes it possible for us to begin to keep the first commandment and to confess "by the power of the Holy Ghost that Jesus is the Christ" (Moroni 7:44) and to have charity. This scriptural insistence on the interactiveness of these virtues deserves real pondering; its recurrence is not accidental.

If one is hopeless, he cannot for long remain sinless, for he will have given up and slackened his resolve; futility fosters vulnerability. The prophets, therefore, say that "without faith there cannot be any hope." (Moroni 7:42.)

Faith, hope, and charity draw to them other needed virtues, such as patience and temperance. We will be abounding in good works if we have faith, hope, and charity (Alma 7:24), because, knowing that there is divine purpose in life and personal accountability, we also know that what we do really matters.

Indeed, this special hope is such that we should be anxious to explain as well as to defend it. So said Peter: "But sanctify the Lord God in your hearts: and *be ready always to give an answer to every man* that asketh you *a reason of the hope that is in you* with meekness and fear." (1 Peter 3:15. Italics added.)

Thus true hope focuses us on the great realities— "things as they really are"— and frees us from unneeded anxiety, but *not* from the necessity of patient endurance. When we are down and discouraged, the hope of Christ can lift us up lest we remain vulnerable overlong. The brisk pace of Church service also helps us focus talent and time outwardly rather than being left alone for long with our moods. Duties knocking at one's door are like friends come to call—not always convenient but usually gladdening in their effect. Our hope rests upon a dependable expectation. Let others, if they choose, define theological hope as a mere wish or an awaiting. Hope includes, in fact, these more passive ingredients. But it is so much more than wishful musing. It stiffens, not slackens, the spine. It is anticipation that turns into day-by-day determination. It is an eager and an enthusiastic expectation based upon a dependable and justifiable object of hope, the triumph of the resurrection-generating Lord Jesus Christ. It is this hope, and this hope alone, that permits us to "endure well" to the end—knowing that the end is but a glorious beginning! It is this same hope that is such a vital and helping virtue when we must "continue the journey" notwithstanding our weaknesses.

We are, therefore, grounded in the *grand hope* that the gospel provides. Our *tactical hopes*, however, are sometimes another matter. We may, for instance, hope to become a doctor or for a certain dating opportunity—outcomes that may not occur in spite of our best efforts. Our hopes of the latter kind, like our prayers, may or may not be granted. If they are not right for us, they may be withheld. If such hopes are subject to the agency of others, and so many are, they may not be realized. But our hopes for the things that really matter will not be blasted by men or circumstance.

If, however, we have this precise and basic hope, insofar as such strategic things as immortality and individuality are concerned, then the spirit of hopefulness will pervade our lives, giving to us a quality of life that is characterized by hopefulness. Real hope also gives us a tactical toughness that befits those who have ultimate hope. Job knew that "my redeemer liveth, and that he shall stand at the latter day upon the earth." (Job 19:25.) Job's hopes did not focus on next year's crops!

If we have this kind of ultimate hope, there is no room for proximate despair. If the big things that really matter are finally going to work out in eternity, then the little things that go wrong mortally are not cause for desperation but perhaps only for a little frustration and irritation.

Ultimate hope and daily grumpiness are clearly not reconcilable. It is ungraceful for a human who has been promised an eternal expanse to be genuinely upset with his family upon coming home from work because someone earlier in the day took his preferred parking place! Likewise, we would say that a farmer who clearly has a bumper crop coming in the fall, and who nevertheless gets upset with a neighbor because the neighbor's pigs got into a small portion of his peapatch in the summer, lacks perspective.

Adults have all seen children foolishly fighting over a

particular doll when other dolls lay nearby but ignored simply because they focused their acquisitiveness on a particular doll at a particular moment. Adult acquisitiveness is less amusing and is even more contagious.

One wonders, even in good people, if peevishness is not one of the last tendencies to be conquered. Littleness in big people is always disappointing. Perhaps such littleness is like litter on an otherwise lovely lawn; we must not be judgmental, of course, but we cannot help noticing. Even so, we'd best look to our own lawns. Hope, on the other hand, encourages a generosity in our human relationships that is consistent with keeping the second commandment.

When disciples are counseled to be of good cheer, we are being instructed about an essential attitude of today that is appropriate for those who have the glorious hopes for eternity. Ultimate hope, if it does not finally dissolve our daily disappointments, at least puts them in perspective.

No wonder as we travel the Lord has told us on many occasions to "be of good cheer" and to "cheer up your hearts." Such cheerfulness will help to insure that we do not become "weary in well-doing." (D&C 64:33.) Part of enduring is to "never be weary of good works." (Alma 37:34.)

Being of good cheer is the opposite of murmuring, complaining, and rebelling during the journey of discipleship. The latter are lapses, and even Father Lehi succumbed on one occasion. (See 1 Nephi 16:25.)

A scriptural survey of murmuring indicates it is equated with complaining. (See 1 Nephi 17:22.) It has occurred in an individual's heart or in groups—out in the open or in the privacy of ancient Israel's tents. Common causes are: resentment at personal chastisement, as with Oliver Cowdery (D&C 9:6); pique at things withheld by the Lord,

as with Emma Smith (D&C 25:4); lack of perspective or because of incomplete information (1 Nephi 2:12; 1 Nephi
16:3; Alma 58); reactions to persecution and fears (Mosiah
27:1; Numbers 14:2; Deuteronomy 1:27); failure to accept
central doctrines and hard sayings (John 6:41, 61; 1 Nephi
16:1-2); and inability to sustain prophetic leaders, such as
Moses and Nephi, which is really rebellion against the Lord
(Exodus 16:8-9; 2 Nephi 5:3).

Other causes of murmuring and complaining range
from thirst for water (Exodus 15:25) to disputes over the
correct name of the Church (3 Nephi 27:4). The former reflected an attitude toward God that could be characterized
by humans saying to God, "What have you done for me
lately?"—and the latter reflected a failure to study and understand the scriptures. Significantly, the scriptures promise that one day the murmurers shall "learn doctrine." (2
Nephi 27:35.)

As we work out our salvation we are to do so without
murmurings, said Paul. (Philippians 2:14.) Thus we, like
the Nephite women, can be, in a sense, toughened, so that
we can "bear [our] journeyings without murmurings." (1
Nephi 17:2.)

While the immediate causes of complaining vary, the
root causes are an unwillingness to trust the Lord's plans or
His teachings or His leaders. Murmurers (and each of us
has no doubt taken a turn at it) have sharp tongues and dull
memories! Perhaps, too, if the journeying Nephite women
can be cited again, we need the equivalent of basic rations
in our diet and less French pastry before we can settle in for
the long journey. We, too, must learn to depend upon the
Lord for our manna and our daily bread, and to be of good
cheer as He leads us along.

Since we can have no justified complaints against the

Lord, who gives us so much, griping simply does not go with gospel gratitude. Ingratitude reflects the intellectual dishonesty of those who can enumerate their grievances but cannot count their blessings.

We must be careful, in this regard, about bringing over into the Church another of the ways of the world: the tendency some have developed to demand that institutions meet their needs. Obviously, the gospel of Jesus Christ and the Church of Jesus Christ do meet our basic needs for happiness here and salvation and eternal life in the world to come. At the same time, some murmur occasionally that the Church must do more "for" such and such a group. There are even touches of demand about certain of these assertions. It is in these attitudes that the danger lies.

The Church is not a democracy that responds to its constituents. We do not make demands of the Lord. Of course, the Church and its leaders at all levels should be sensitive to conditions in the Church—if for no other reason than the keeping of the second commandment—but, most of all, as shepherds of the flock. But, as we have so sadly learned in recent secular and political history, a preferential program is seldom the "cure" for a basic need.

Rather, all solutions and all joy are bound up in the individual keeping of His commandments and the doing of our duties. There is a difference, therefore, between the importuning widow and the strident murmurings of ancient Israel in the Sinai. After all, it is we who are to adapt in order to follow the Lord's ways, not the other way around.

Happily, the same regularized hopefulness can also see us through far more stressful difficulties such as funerals, where we seem to take turns. Sometimes we're on the stand. Mostly we're in the audience. Sooner or later, however, almost all of us end up on the first row with the special opportunities for deep reflection which that wrenching experience can bring.

It is in these crunches of life—whether in temptation or trial—that it becomes most clear whether or not we really have gospel hope. If the deceased has run with patience the race set before him, he or she has triumphed, and, though perhaps drained by affliction, that person can now be filled everlastingly. Thus, while at a funeral we mourn deeply and openly, given gospel hope we also celebrate sincerely and quietly. Interrelationships have been interrupted, but only briefly. Resumption for the righteous is guaranteed by the resurrection.

In understanding and accepting the Lord's plan, there is a need for such hope, for we do not all die quietly in our sleep of heart attacks at age ninety. Some go so young, some so grindingly. Some go so long after they wish to. The scriptures that counsel us to confess God's hand in all things need to be understood in the context that God has clearly not caused all suffering—but He has surely taken it into account in His plans. And he has seen to it that His grace (which undergirds our hope) is sufficient for the righteous.

All of us who will—all of us who are truly hopeful—are being fitted in this life for duties elsewhere, very demanding duties. Therefore, our schooling here cannot be casual. When our anguish and pain here are over, the added compassion and empathy we have thus developed will last for eternity. So often it seems that those who already have empathy are made the more so by suffering. Should it surprise us, however, to see the good become very good? Only they are really ready for such next steps, just as only the good really know about temptation.

Some who have a brightness of hope live their last days

in a circumstance described by a prophet as one in which "there is but a step between me and death." (1 Samuel 20:3.) That step between life and death permits those individuals who are filled with hope to do and say a number of important things in their remaining time. Being so self-sufficient and so helping of others, such disciples do not wish to become a burden. Being a burden becomes a special burden, suggesting, perhaps, that for those who know full well how blessed it is to give, it is now necessary to know how blessed it is to receive. We create each other's opportunities for giving—like it or not! Hope-filled souls do not crave affliction or seeming tragedy, but they will use all such circumstances for their eternal good.

On the other side of the veil, there are perhaps seventy billion people. They need the same gospel, and releases occur here to aid the Lord's work there. Each release of a righteous individual from this life is also a call to new labors. Those who have true hope understand this.

Therefore, though we miss the departed righteous so much here, hundreds may feel their touch there. One day, those hundreds will thank the bereaved for gracefully forgoing the extended association with choice individuals here, in order that they could help hundreds there. In God's ecology, talent and love are never wasted. The hopeful understand this, too.

Our tears, therefore, when we weep for the departed righteous, are not tears of despair. Mingled among these tears are also the tears of our anticipation and justified hope of the glorious reunions that await. The Lord Himself has said our empathy and anguish are both approved and appropriate: "Thou shalt live together in love, insomuch that thou shalt weep for the loss of them that die." But when we weep, the Lord added, weep "more especially for those that have not hope of a glorious resurrection." (D&C 42:45.) Ironically, the general resurrection that disbelievers choose to ignore will mercifully not ignore them.

The scriptures declare that "precious in the sight of the Lord is the death of his saints" (Ps. 116:15), and that "the last enemy that shall be destroyed is death" (1 Corinthians 15:26). Death and time will exit together from our experience, no more to return.

A tender and hope-filled assurance is given by Isaiah, who said the Savior "will swallow up death in victory; and the Lord God will wipe away tears from off all faces." (Isaiah 25:8.) The Lord, who knows perfectly about suffering, will, one day, comfort us so personally. The hopeful understand this as well.

In Mosiah, we read about how sainthood is to be obtained not only by the cultivation of cardinal and hard-won virtues such as love and patience, but also by the development of a special "willingness" that is described to us in a soul-shivering verse—a willingness "to submit to all the things which the Lord seeth fit to inflict" upon us. (Mosiah 3:19.) This willingness is the unconditional submittal of our souls to Him whose love of us, individually, is unconditional and perfect. Those who can so trust God and who see His hand in all things can effect such a submittal with a "brightness of hope."

As our turns come to be on the front row at funerals, therefore, let us be likewise restrained amid our anguish, for hope can help us avoid becoming hostages of despair. Hope also can keep us from charging God foolishly! (See Job 1:22.) Later it will turn out, so far as the allocation of certain afflictions is concerned, that we owe God not accusation, but deep, deep appreciation!

When the plan of salvation was presented to us, we had

a correct and hope-filled perspective, for we are reliably told that we "shouted for joy." (Job 38:7.) Our lives today ought to echo the cheerfulness of that ancient shout, because none of the fundamental reasons for our rejoicing then have changed since.

Jesus will return in triumph, ere long, to usher in a millennial reign of peace on earth. The glorious resurrection is guaranteed to us all unconditionally. A better world will then envelop us all. But these basic blessings must be distinguished from the disappointments of the day; these eternal realities may be obscured.

An economic depression would be grim, but it would not change the reality of immortality. The inevitability of the second coming is not affected by the unpredictability of the stock market. Political despots make this world very ugly, but they cannot touch that better world to come. A case of cancer does not cancel the promises of the temple endowment.

Thus the things of which we can be most certain are also those things which matter most. We can cheerfully say with Job that "my redeemer liveth, and that he shall stand at the latter day upon the earth." (Job 19:25.) Suffering Job did not, however, pin his hopes on having bumper crops next year or getting back his lost sheep and camels. So it should be with us. We can have a bad day but still have a good life. We can have tribulation but see it paled by the resurrection. We can exhibit calm commitment as did hope-filled Job amid tribulation and avoid charging "God foolishly." (Job 1:22.)

Thus, nothing that really matters has changed since long ago when, with full justification, we shouted for joy. All that matters is gloriously intact. The promises are in place. It is up to us to perform.

Someday when we kneel again in those corridors where that special shout once echoed, having been delivered from our last enemy, death, we will have hearts "swollen with joy, unto the gushing out of many tears." (3 Nephi 4:33.) It is a moment we must not miss! It is worth cheerfully enduring a few disappointments and pains now and letting a few mortal appetites go unsated.

Meanwhile, especially when we are happy, we should not be surprised that time passes so quickly. It was so with Jacob, who worked to earn Rachel: ". . . and they seemed unto him but a few days, for the love he had to her." (Genesis 29:20.) Let us cheerfully use the "few days" each of us have left here.

Hope is, therefore, a functional and a cardinal virtue. Indeed, though it may seem otherwise at times, proximate and ultimate hope are really one true hope—tied to one Lord, Jesus Christ.

Hope does the seeing, albeit through glass darkly, but it is patience that sees us through.

# 4

## *Patience*

The absolute necessity of our having the intriguing attribute of patience is cited several times in the scriptures, including by King Benjamin, who clustered the attributes of a saint, and *patience* was a charter member. (Mosiah 3:19. See also Alma 7:23.) Patience is not only one of the virtues resulting from being a true believer in Christ, it is also an essential factor in the process of bringing about all the other virtues. Indeed, patience is especially essential for those of us who have been called to His work notwithstanding our weaknesses. Like hope, patience is a virtue that deserves much more reflection and attention than it usually receives. Furthermore, some of us want patience but we want it right now!

Patience is not to be mistaken for indifference. It is to care very much, but to be willing, nevertheless, to submit both to the Lord and to what the scriptures call the "process of time."

Patience is tied very closely to other essential attributes such as *faith* and *hope* in our Heavenly Father and Jesus Christ. (1 Timothy 6:11.) When we are unduly impatient with circumstances, we may be suggesting that we know what is best—better than does God. Or, at least, we are asserting that our timeable is better than His. Either way, we are questioning the reality of God's omniscience as if, as some seem to believe, God were on some sort of post-doctoral fellowship, trying to complete His understanding and, therefore, needing to use us as consultants.

We read in Mosiah about how the Lord simultaneously tries, randomly, the patience of His people even as He tries their faith. (Mosiah 23:21.) One is not only to endure, but to endure well and gracefully, those things that the Lord "seeth fit to inflict" upon us (Mosiah 3:19), just as did a group of ancient American saints who were bearing unusual burdens but who submitted "cheerfully and with patience to all the will of the Lord" (Mosiah 24:15).

Paul, speaking to the Hebrews, brings us up short by writing that even after faithful disciples had "done the will of God," they had need of patience. (Hebrews 10:36.) How many times have good individuals done the right thing only to break, or wear away, under the subsequent stress, canceling out much of the value of what they have already so painstakingly done?

Sometimes that which we are doing is correct enough but simply needs to be persisted in—patiently—not for a minute or a moment, but sometimes for years. Paul speaks of the marathon of life and how we must "run with patience the race that is set before us." (Hebrews 12:1.) Paul did not select for his analogy the hundred yard dash!

The Lord has said: "And seek the face of the Lord always, that *in patience ye may possess your souls*, and ye shall have eternal life." (D&C 101:38. Italics added. See also Luke 21:19.) Could it be that only when our self-control has become total do we come into true possession of our own souls?

Patience is not only a companion of faith, but is also a

friend of *free agency*. Inside our impatience there is sometimes an ugly reality: we are plainly irritated and inconve-
nienced by the need to make allowances for the free agency
of others. In our impatience, which is not the same thing as
divine discontent, we would override others, even though
it is obvious that our individual differences and preferences
are so irretrievably enmeshed with each other that the only
resolution that preserves free agency is for us to be patient
and longsuffering with each other, notwithstanding our
weaknesses.

The passage of time is not, by itself, an automatic cure
for bad choices. But often individuals, like the prodigal
son, can "in process of time" come to their senses. The
touching reunion of Jacob and Esau in the desert, so many
years after their youthful rivalry, is a classic example of
how generosity can replace animosity when truth is mixed
with time.

When we are unduly impatient, however, we are, in effect, trying to hasten an outcome when acceleration would
abuse agency. Enoch, brilliant, submissive, and spiritual,
knew what it meant to see a whole city-culture advance "in
process of time." He could tell us so much about so many
things, including patience.

Patience makes possible a personal spiritual symmetry
that arises only from prolonged *obedience within free agency*.
There is also a dimension of patience that links it to a special
*reverence for life*. Patience is a willingness, in a sense, to
watch the unfolding purposes of God with a sense of
wonder and awe—rather than pacing up and down within
the cell of our circumstance.

Too much anxious opening of the oven door and the
cake falls instead of rising. So it is with us. If we are always
selfishly taking our temperature to see if we are happy, we

won't be. When we are impatient, we are neither reveren-
tial nor reflective, because we are too self-centered. Whereas faith and patience are companions, so are selfishness
and impatience.

It is so easy to be confrontive without being informative;
indignant without being intelligent; impulsive without being insightful. It is so easy to command others when we are
not in control of ourselves. Patience helps us to view imperfections in others more generously to the end that we may
learn to be more wise than they have been. (See Mormon
9:31.)

Even so, Job did not make the mistake of charging God
foolishly. (See Job 1:22.) Life was flowing rather smoothly
for Job until the trials came to him, prior to which the adversary saw him as having a protective "hedge about him."
(Job 1:10.) The challenges of life came with an intensity and
on a scale that he had never before known. Yet the Lord
had confidence in him, based not only upon His observa-
tions of Job in this life but, in fact, in the world before. Surely Job was one of those of whom a Book of Mormon prophet
was speaking when he said that some were ordained—"being called and prepared from the foundation of the world
according to the foreknowledge of God, on account of their
exceeding faith and good works." (Alma 13:3.)

James stressed the importance of patience when our
faith is being tried, because those grueling experiences
"worketh patience"; he said, in what was almost a sigh of
the soul, "let patience have her perfect work." (James
1:3-4.)

To Joseph Smith, the Lord described patience as having
a special finishing or concluding role, for "these things remain to be overcome through patience, that such may receive an exceeding and eternal weight of glory." (D&C

63:66.) A patient disciple will not be surprised or undone when the Church is misrepresented.

Peter, being toughminded as well as tender, made the test of our patience even more precise and demanding when he said, "For what glory is it, if, when ye be buffeted for your faults, ye shall take it patiently? but if, when ye do well, and suffer for it, ye take it patiently, this is acceptable with God." (1 Peter 2:20.) The dues of discipleship are high indeed, and how much we can *take* so often determines how much we can then *give*!

Thus, as already indicated, patience is a vital virtue in relation to our faith, our free agency, our attitude toward life, our humility, and our suffering. Moreover, patience will not be an obsolete attribute in the next world!

The longer one examines the gospel of Jesus Christ, the more he will understand that the Lord's commitment to free agency is very, very deep—so much deeper than is our own. The more one lives, the more he will also sense how exquisite is God's perfect love of us. It is, in fact, the very interplay of God's everlasting commitment to free agency and His everlasting and perfect love for us that inevitably places a high premium upon the virtue of patience. There is, given our weaknesses, simply no other way for true growth to occur.

Do we not get a breathtaking glimpse of God's perfect patience in the execution of the plan of salvation, again and again, concerning which He has said his course "is one eternal round"? (D&C 3:2.)

Thus it is that patience is to human nature what photosynthesis is to nature. Photosynthesis, the most important single chemical reaction, brings together water, light, chlorophyll, and carbon dioxide, processing annually the hundreds of trillions of tons of carbon dioxide, converting them to oxygen as part of the process of making food and fuel. The marvelous process of photosynthesis is crucial to life on this planet, and it is a very constant and patient process. So, too, is an individual's spiritual growth.

Patience is always involved in the spiritual chemistry of life—not only when we try to turn trials and tribulations, the carbon dioxide, as it were, into joy and growth, but it also builds upon the seemingly ordinary experiences to bring about happy, spiritual outcomes. (Neither patience nor photosynthesis is a conspicuous process.)

Patience is, therefore, clearly not fatalistic, shoulder-shrugging resignation; it is accepting a divine rhythm to life; it is obedience prolonged. Patience stoutly resists pulling up the daisies to see how the roots are doing!

Patience, when combined with love and regard for others, will help us greatly in the relationships of the generations and in how we view the mistakes of parents or those who may have preceded us, as is eloquently embodied in these words: "Condemn me not because of mine imperfection, neither my father, because of his imperfection, neither them who have written before him; but rather give thanks unto God that he hath made manifest unto you our imperfections, that ye may learn to be more wise than we have been." (Mormon 9:31.)

Patience will also see us through troubles, because of the perspective that patience brings. A patient Paul declared, "We are troubled on every side, yet not distressed; we are perplexed, but not in despair; Persecuted, but not forsaken; cast down but not destroyed." (2 Corinthians 4:8-9.)

The author remembers as a child going eagerly to the corner store for what we then called the "all-day sucker." It would not have lasted all day under the best of usage, but it could last quite a while. The trick was to resist the temptation to bite into it, to learn to savor rather than to crunch and chew. The same savoring was needed with a precious square of milk chocolate. Make the treat last, especially in depression times!

In life, however, even patiently stretching out sweetness is sometimes not enough; in certain situations, enjoyment must actually be deferred. A patient willingness to defer dividends is a hallmark of individual maturity. It is, parenthetically, a hallmark of free nations that their citizens can discipline themselves today for a better tomorrow. Yet America is in trouble (as are other nations) because the patient persistence in a wise course of public policy now appears to be so difficult to attain. Too many impatient politicians buy today's votes with tomorrow's inflation.

But back to the personal relevance of patience, which, among many things, permits us to deal more effectively with the unevenness of life's experiences.

The seeming flat periods of life give us a blessed chance to reflect upon what is past as well as to be readied for some rather stirring climbs ahead. Patience helps us to use, rather than to protest, these seeming flat periods of life, becoming filled with quiet wonder over the past and with anticipation for that which may lie ahead. Instead of grumbling and murmuring, we should be consolidating and reflecting, which would simply not happen if life were an uninterrupted sequence of fantastic scenery, confrontive events, or exhilarating conversation.

We should savor even the seemingly ordinary times, for life cannot be made up of all kettledrums and crashing cymbals. There must be some flutes and violins. Living cannot be all crescendo; there must be some counterpoint.

Clearly, without patience we will learn less in life. We will see less. We will feel less. We will hear less. Ironically, "rush" and "more" usually mean "less." The pressures of "now," time and time again, go against the grain of the gospel with its eternalism.

There is also in patience a greater opportunity for that discernment which sorts out the things that matter most from the things that matter least.

In our approach to life, patience also helps us to realize that while we may be ready to move on, having had enough of a particular learning experience, our continuing presence is often a needed part of the learning environment of others. Patience is thus closely connected with two other central attributes of Christianity—love and humility.

Paul said to the saints at Thessalonica, "Be patient toward all men," clearly a part of keeping the second commandment. (1 Thessalonians 5:14.)

A patient person assumes that what others have to say is worth listening to. A patient person is not so chronically eager to put forth his or her own ideas. In true humility, we do some waiting upon others. We value them for what they say and what they have to contribute. Patience and humility are special friends.

Since our competition in life, as Elder Boyd K. Packer has perceptively said, is solely with our old self, we ought to be free of the jealousies and anxieties of the world that go with interpersonal competition. Very importantly, it is patience, combined with love, that permits us "in process of time," to detoxify our disappointments. Patience and love take the radioactivity out of our resentments. These are neither small nor occasional needs in most of our lives!

Further, the patient person can better understand how there are circumstances when, if our hearts are set too

much upon the things of this world, they must be broken—
but for our sakes and not merely as a demonstration of divine power. But it takes real patience in such circumstances
to wait for the later vindication of our trust in the Lord.

Therefore, if we use the process of time well, it can cradle us as we develop patient humility. Keats tenderly observed: "Time, that aged nurse,/Rock'd me to patience."
(*Endymion*, bk. 1, l. 705.)

Clearly, patience so cradles us amidst *suffering*. Paul,
who had suffered much, observed in his epistle to the Hebrews: "Now no chastening for the present seemeth to be
joyous, but grievous: nevertheless afterward it yieldeth the
peaceable fruit of righteousness unto them which are exercised thereby." (Hebrews 12:11.)

Patience permits us to cling to our faith in the Lord
when we are tossed about by suffering as if by surf. When
the undertow grasps us, we will realize that we are somehow being carried forward even as we tumble; we are actually being helped even as we cry for help.

One of the functions of the tribulation of the righteous is
so that "tribulation worketh patience." (Romans 5:3.) What
a vital attribute patience is if tribulation is worth enduring
to bring about its development!

Patience in turn brings about needed experience, as
noted in the stunning insight the Lord gave to the Prophet
Joseph Smith: "All these things shall give thee experience,
and shall be for thy good." (D&C 121:7.) Perhaps one can
be forgiven if, in response to this sobering insight, his soul
shivers just a bit.

In life, the sandpaper of circumstances often smooths
our crustiness and patiently polishes our rough edges.
There is nothing pleasant about it, however. And the Lord
will go to great lengths in order to teach us a particular les-

son and to help us to overcome a particular weakness, especially if there is no other way. In such circumstances, it is quite useless for us mortals to try to do our own sums when it comes to suffering. We can't make it all add up because clearly we do not have all the numbers. Furthermore, none of us knows much about the algebra of affliction. The challenges that come are shaped to our needs and circumstances, sometimes in order to help our weaknesses become strengths. Job noted how tailored his challenges were, saying, "For the thing which I greatly feared has come upon me, and that which I was afraid of is come unto me." (Job 3:25.) Yet he prevailed—so much so that he was held up as a model to the great latter-day prophet, Joseph Smith. (D&C 121.) Our triumph here could not be complete if we merely carried our fears and doubts into the next world. What came to Job was not a minor test with which he could have coped with one hand tied behind him. Rather, "his grief was very great." (Job 2:13.)

Thus, when we are patiently growing and keeping the commandments of God and doing our duties, we are to that extent succeeding, a fact from which we should derive some quiet, inner reassurance. Knowing that we are in the process of succeeding, even though we have much to do and much to improve upon, can help us to move forward, while, at the same time, being "of good cheer." Setting a correct pattern in our lives is vital, but so is patient persistence in that pattern. Like it or not, the journey we have undertaken simply cannot be made without patience. Patience can be the spiritual equivalent of photosynthesis as it helps to turn our weaknesses into strengths.

In the divine developmental process we do not become saints in a season. We do not usually even fully finish putting off the natural man that quickly, given our weaknesses. The "mighty change" takes patience, but it is a grave error to postpone the putting off.

# 5

## *Put Off the Natural Man and Become a Saint*

There are those who, reading certain scriptural descriptions about the nature of man (such as that man is "carnal, sensual, and devilish," Alma 42:10) brush by these scriptures hurriedly, even nervously, because they feel so uncomfortable upon reading them. Such readers may feel, wrongly, that these scriptures sound much like a Calvinistic denigration of man. Such offended readers may even say those adjectives do not sound like most of the people they know. The same brush-by occurs regarding the numerous scriptures concerning "darkness" and "light."

There is a danger, however, in ignoring these scriptures and the profound message they contain. Calvinism focused *unnaturally* on the *natural* man and lacked the lifting dimension contained in the fullness of the gospel of Jesus Christ, with its exalting perspectives and sweeping promises. Though these scriptural insights concerning the natural man may seem to put us sternly in our place, when they are combined with the fullness of the gospel, we are shown our immense possibilities and what we have the power to become. Are we not wiser to understand our fallen nature and then, with equal attention, to be taught about how we can be lifted up? Indeed, for one to ask "Where do we go from here?" he must know where "here" is!

Furthermore, just as Calvinism in its lack of completeness put mankind down, there occurred, in subsequent reaction thereto, an almost unbridled secular-religious optimism about man and his possibilities. Because it, too, was incomplete, this optimism went sour, as secular hopes have a way of doing.

The fullness of the gospel of Jesus Christ, however, with its interwoven and related truths, gives us precious balance about our true nature, including how natural men can become "partakers of the divine nature." (2 Peter 1:4.)

Let us, therefore, pause and examine the "natural man" and seek to understand what it is that we must put off.

First of all, the natural man is an "enemy to God." (Mosiah 3:19.) This means that such individuals would (whether fully understanding the implications of their own resistance or not) oppose the ultimate purpose of God for mankind, which is, as we know, "to bring to pass the immortality and eternal life of man." (Moses 1:39.) Given our eternal interests, the natural man therefore is not our friend either, even if, at times, we seem quite at home with him.

The natural man is intellectually proud, excluding divine data and counsel that are essential to our welfare. The Lord speaks of how those who "seek not the Lord to establish his righteousness" and who are, therefore, disposed to create a circumstance in which "every man walketh in his own way, and after the image of his own god, whose image is in the likeness of the world." (D&C 1:16.)

Instead of becoming a saint, being childlike and willing to submit to our eternal Father, the natural man is rebellious and insists on walking in his own way. He is childish instead of childlike.

The natural man also stubbornly seeks for happiness in

iniquity—an incredibly naive notion about the nature of happiness and the universe. We read this of such souls: "But behold, your days of probation are past; ye have procrastinated the day of your salvation until it is everlastingly too late, and your destruction is made sure; yea, for ye have *sought* all the days of your lives *for that which ye could not obtain*; and ye have sought *for happiness in doing iniquity*, which thing is contrary to the nature of that righteousness which is in our great and Eternal Head." (Helaman 13:38. Italics added.)

Thus it is that the natural man, in attempting to live "without God in the world" and in catering slavishly to his natural instincts, is actually living "contrary to the nature of happiness." (Alma 41:11.)

Being selfish, natural man will abuse authority and power whether political, economic, or whatever: "We have learned by sad experience that it is the nature and disposition of *almost all* men, as soon as they get a little authority, as they suppose, they will immediately begin to exercise unrighteous dominion." (D&C 121:39. Italics added.)

"Almost all" is an awful indictment! One's rejection of this insight will not alter the history of "sad experience." Those who think of themselves as clear and obvious exceptions to this rule are the least likely so to be.

Paul described the natural man as given over to the lusts of the flesh and also as inclined to wrath, no doubt borne of the strong ego drive that, in the beginning, insists that he stubbornly walk in his own way: "Wherein in time past ye walked according to the course of this world, according to the prince of the power of the air, the spirit that now worketh in the children of disobedience: Among whom also we all had our conversation in times past in the lusts of our flesh, fulfilling the desires of the flesh and of the mind;

and were *by nature the children of wrath*, even as others."
(Ephesians 2:2-3. Italics added.)

Indeed, as individuals on a large enough scale become
depraved and overcome with darkness, symptoms such as
those described in the ninth chapter of Moroni do appear in
which such individuals, indeed whole societies, have "lost
their love, one towards another," and are "without order,"
"without mercy," "without civilization," "strong in their
perversion," and "past feeling."

Is it too strong, therefore, to describe such individuals
as being "carnal, sensual, and devilish"? If their purposes
do not accord with those of God, then they are to that extent devilish. To the extent that they are strong in their perversions, they surely must be described as sensual. To the
extent that they are acting contrary to the nature of their
own happiness in the lusts of the flesh, they surely must be
described as carnal. When a diagnosis is accurate, we had
best accept it, for accepting can be the beginning of both
treatment and wisdom.

It should not surprise us that such coarse, spiritually
unrefined individuals cannot receive the things of the Spirit but are shut out from the very light that could show them,
if they were willing, how to put off the natural man. The
seeming shutters on the windows of heaven are but the
natural scales on our own eyes. Paul said it well: "But the
natural man receiveth not the things of the Spirit of God:
for they are foolishness unto him: neither can he know
them, because they are spiritually discerned." (1 Corinthians 2:14.)

Therefore, only to the extent that we are willing to put
off the natural man do we have any real hope at all of becoming saints. It is the putting off of the putting off that is
our real problem, however.

Letting go of the world requires not only deliberate disengagement from the ways of the world, but also being willing to take the next step by yielding to the enticings of the Spirit. If one refuses to do both things, the prognosis is poor, for our childish rebellion will continue. "But remember that he that persists in his own carnal nature, and goes on in the ways of sin and rebellion against God, remaineth in his fallen state and the devil hath all power over him. Therefore, he is as though there was no redemption made, being an enemy to God; and also is the devil an enemy to God." (Mosiah 16:5.)

So far as our real self-interests are concerned, sin is irrational even when measured merely in the dimenson of time. It is insanity when viewed by the eyes of eternity. Of course, the adversary's trick is to make that which hurts us seem pleasing and that which is ugly seem attractive. Such huckstering requires real cleverness—but, most of all, credulous consumers. Discerning consumerism is currently much urged in the marketplace of goods, but it is regarded as out of place in the bazaar of behavior!

If, however, one can begin to understand his position in this world and his relationship to our Heavenly Father, even though he may have previously spent much time as a patron in "Vanity Fair," it is not too late, as the earlier-quoted words of Malcolm Muggeridge attest.

When we begin to put off the natural man and move, however slightly, toward sainthood, we will find ourselves almost at once beginning to be stretched conceptually. It becomes possible for us to know things we did not believe it possible to know. "And now behold, my brethren, what natural man is there that knoweth these things? I say unto you, there is none that knoweth these things, save it be the penitent." (Alma 26:21.)

We thus become eligible to receive "the things of the Spirit of God" which the natural man cannot receive. (See 1 Corinthians 2:14.)

The greater our yielding to the enticings of the Spirit, the more we are stretched conceptually and experientially. This was the case with Moses, who was highly developed spiritually. Being shown by God His creations, Moses declared that he had been shown things which he "never had supposed." (Moses 1:10.)

When Moses observed after this marvelous experience that "man is nothing," this surely was not a reflection on man, "God's greatest miracle," but a placing of man in the vast perspective of God's creations and a realizing, even so, that we are God's exclusive work and his greatest glory. What a marvelous rejoinder Moses' vision is to those who superficially seize upon adjectives like *carnal, sensual,* and *devilish* as a means of excusing themselves from any effort to be otherwise!

Only to the extent that we put off the natural man can we eventually abide the presence of God and see Him. (See D&C 67:10-12.) Likewise, only when we put off the natural man and become saints can we then have access to the powers of heaven and handle them properly. No longer would we then use power and authority to "cover our sins" or to "gratify our pride, or our vain ambition." No longer would we "exercise control or dominion or compulsion upon the souls of the children of men, in any degree of unrighteousness." (D&C 121:37.) Who would care to tally the misery in human history resulting from the unrighteous use of power, whether in peer pressures or dictatorships? Rather, having so qualified by responding to the "enticings of the Spirit" we would find that "the Holy Ghost shall be thy constant companion, and thy scepter an unchanging scepter of righteousness and truth; and thy dominion shall be *an everlasting dominion,* and *without compulsory means* it shall flow unto thee forever and ever." (D&C 121:46. Italics added.) Only as we become partakers of the divine nature are we qualified to become partakers of divine power.

Furthermore, as we progress in this manner spiritually, we will not only confess God's hands in all things and do so gladly, but we will also be able to connect correct concepts and to see how *all* His commandments are spiritual. (See D&C 29:35.)

Saintlike individuals seem to be so rare that we have almost ceased thinking about what living in a society of saints would be like. Such a people existed for several decades. There was real peace, real freedom, prosperity without poverty, an absence of envy, lying, violence, whoredoms, and lasciviousness; "surely there could not be a happier people." (4 Nephi 1:16.)

Some may freely say that they do not wish to meet the terms set down by God for achieving such ideal conditions. But given the fact that God *is* there and these *are* His terms, we are not able to reorder these realities of universe to multiply the options. Our choice is to seek to establish His righteousness or to rebelliously continue to walk in our own way.

We are free to choose, to obey or not to obey, to come to terms or not to come to terms with the Lord. But we cannot revise the terms. And even the refusal to come to terms with God will, ere long, be an option no longer open, for every knee will bow and every tongue will confess that Jesus is the Christ. Even those who have lived without God in the world will finally confess that God has dealt justly with them. (See Mosiah 16:1.)

Once we have come to terms, however, then come the

steps toward sainthood. And mere steps they are, as we learn to become submissive, humble, meek, patient, and full of love. (Mosiah 3:19.)

This process of putting off and becoming, however, requires the constant light of the gospel so that we can see and understand what we are doing.

One recurring theme of the gospel (with the commandments representing light and evil representing darkness) raises an interesting possibility, namely, that (with some exceptions) those who sin do so because they are in that darkness which envelops the natural man. Had they been in light and had they been able to foresee the multiple and awful consequences of their sins, they usually would not have done what they did! Unfortunately, the morning after does not occur the day before.

Perhaps it is too strong to say that sin reflects a temporary form of insanity, but it is at least correct to say that when we are in darkness, even if momentary, we do not in the darkness see clearly the consequences of our acts. Would the tempted father commit adultery, knowing what it might do to his wife and children as well as to other victims if he could, at the moment of decision, foresee clearly how very much those moments of so-called pleasure would cost him? Many, if their confessions are any indication, later regard such moments as moments of great foolishness and stupidity and are scarcely able to understand how it happened that they fell. Enlightened self-interest requires light. Without light, reason soon degenerates into rationalization. Nor does the multiplication of our rationalizations increase their validity—only their availability. But since the process of rationalization holds real peril, it deserves some comment.

First of all, those confronted by *large* temptations *usually* got there by "setting themselves up" in *small* ways. Their dalliance has already caused them to look the other way as some guerrillas are let into the palace grounds of the soul. This compromised condition (unlike the temptations that confront the Savior, which were real but which were dispatched summarily) brings on a second: a weakened capacity to cope, not only because resolve has become flaccid, but because some light has departed when it was needed most and some darkness has entered in. As things worsen, the possible victim is, therefore, not at his best—neither spiritually nor intellectually. He is not yet helpless, but he will clearly need help from heaven in order to avoid *enormous errors* that are now possible because of *small stupidities*.

The sad but interesting thing about step-by-step rationalization is, whether we recognize it or not, that when we take the second and third wrong steps without halting, we hardly notice the forty-third or forty-fourth steps.

The gradualness of it all does not make us less accountable, however, for we are relentlessly moving away from light and into darkness of our own accord; we are still failing to heed what warning signs there are. It is, alas, just that becoming oblivious to these remaining signs is more understandable in the gathering dusk.

The author listened recently to a case wherein a deserting father had listed numerous reasons *against* his leaving and only one *for* his leaving; he mistakenly concluded the one outweighed all the others, and that it alone really mattered. A single appetite had darkened his intellect. The reasoning that went on would be amusing if its consequences had not been so serious. Pottage comes in many forms, but each mess responds to appetites—like lust, hunger, status, wealth, praise, and so forth. It is in the darkness of dimmed perceptivity that such an appetite can cause us, like Esau, to despise our birthright (Genesis 25:34) and to surrender our possibilities. Succumbing to temptation is, therefore, not the result of one's being grossly overprogrammed, but of grossly undervaluing oneself!

Even when we are not confronted with major *temptation* but merely *irritation*, the temporary darkening of our minds desensitizes us and blocks from our view the consequences of an intemperate word—consequences we would otherwise not wish to create. It is the same irrationality all over again, the acting against our own interests, as well as the interests of others.

There are, to be sure, those who love the darkness more than light, but for most, their deviations into darkness are not usually a thought-through venture.

Hence walking in the light becomes incredibly important. Things that assist us so to do, such as deliberate and appropriate associational patterns, doing our duties, and so forth, are to be much valued, not because they themselves are a primary source of light, but because they keep us in the light. Thus the writer of Proverbs was clearly attuned when he wrote, "For the commandment is a lamp; and the law is light." (Proverbs 6:23.)

The adversary will persuade all he can to rage against that which is light and good. (See 2 Nephi 28:20.) Thus it is that the better some become, the more likely it is they will experience (at different times and at different hands) suffering "for the name of Christ," and "as a Christian." (1 Peter 4:14-16.) To be sure, there are many decent and good people in the earth who both do and admire good works and righteousness. But there are others who will, like the prince of darkness, rage against light and that which is good.

Even in dark times, however, the light of the gospel can persist whether it is within an individual or a household. The reader will recall how in God's retributions on the rulers and people of Egypt, there was "darkness over the land of Egypt, even darkness which may be felt." This especially thick darkness lasted three days. The people of Egypt could not even see one another in the deep darkness, and they apparently remained immobile. However, "all the children of Israel had light in their dwellings." (Exodus 10:21-23.) It can and must be so in our time as we strive to have "love at home" and light in our dwellings regardless of that which is without.

Jesus warned us that evildoers hate light that illuminates their iniquity. (See John 3:20.) Some foolishly think that if they merely cover their eyes, they can cover their sins.

We lessen the light, however, when we focus on only a portion of the gospel to the exclusion of any other part. The truths of the gospel of Jesus Christ belong to each other. To focus on one commandment to the exclusion of another can cause doctrinal distortion and behavioral incompleteness. One cannot take from the gospel of Jesus Christ a single truth and have it prosper. Some have so tried in vain with the so-called social gospel, and others, to their sorrow, with apostate variants of marriage. We need the wholeness of the gospel to make us whole.

While the doctrines of the kingdom are simple, they are powerful enough first to shake and then restructure our view of self, life, and the universe. When they are held together in a steady state, they are safe and redemptive. Let one split apart, however, and it becomes dangerous. Doctrines that spin off from all the rest are often used by the adversary for his purposes, since the more truth an error contains, the more dangerous it is. Hence the simple but vital ground rules and the safety slogans we see constantly posted—ground rules such as "only the prophet can receive revelation for the Church," and "no personal interpretation will come that is contrary to the teachings of the living prophet."

In addition to the safety markers, there are other safeguards, such as periodic interviews, and home and visiting teachers being anxiously engaged in the doing of our duties. Even so, tragedies occur, as he who deluded himself so terribly in an earlier estate gets the unwary to delude themselves, or he induces a slackness in the safeguard system as sentries who should call a halt grow weary, waving on the very individuals who should be stopped for the sake of their souls.

As further evidence of the Lord's use of the analogy of light and darkness, we note that there are several scriptural references to circumstances in which individuals' minds are described as having been darkened. (See D&C 10:2; 84:54, 80.)

It is possible, noted the Lord, for such individuals to be "walking in darkness at noon-day." (D&C 95:6.) How does this condition arise? Quite simply: "If you keep not my commandments, the love of the Father shall not continue with you, therefore you shall walk in darkness." (D&C 95:12.) It is not that God ceases to love the sinner (though despising his deeds); it is that the sinner ceases to love God—and the darkness deepens.

There are still other scriptural references to individuals who "love darkness rather than light." (See D&C 10:21; 29:45.) When, however, we reach a certain point—when our eye is single to God's glory—we will be "filled with light, and there shall be no darkness" in us, "and that body which is filled with light comprehendeth all things." (D&C 88:67.) Note, however, that the continued presence in us of light and truth clearly depends upon our keeping that first great commandment.

Paul discussed alienation from the life of God that results from darkened understanding through ignorance, because of "the blindness of their heart." Paul then noted that such individuals were desensitized, because in their celebration of sensuality, they had "given themselves over unto lasciviousness." (Ephesians 4:18-19.) He concluded: "Ye are all the children of light, and the children of the day: we are not of the night, nor of darkness." (1 Thessalonians 5:5.) There is nothing in the night, therefore, that will encourage us to put off the natural man. But everything about light so insists on our pressing forward toward becoming saints!

Not only must each of us so change, but to keep fully the second commandment, we must help others do likewise. This requires us to perform practical duties such as friendshipping and fellowshipping, since we can make no greater contribution to another mortal than to help him become worthy of eternal life, which is God's greatest gift. This involves us, inevitably, in work for both the living and the dead.

We must be more ready than we now are to receive the hundreds of thousands of converts who are putting off the natural man and are coming into the light—from all circumstances, heralding what President Spencer W. Kimball has called an era of major growth for the Church. This scripture will be worth even more pondering in the days ahead: "Again, the kingdom of heaven is like unto a net, that was cast into the sea, and gathered of every kind." (Matthew 13:47.)

Some will have said to their dark past, their behavioral Babylons, "We bid thee farewell." They have learned that without the decalog there is decadence.

Other newcomers will have learned that it is not good for man to be alone, and will have ceased trying to live without God in the world. (See Alma 41:11.)

Still others will come out of the kingdom of the devil, which the Lord, as promised, will shake in order to stir some therein to repentance. (See 2 Nephi 28:19.) From such tumblings, souls come to us bruised but believing, having made their way courageously through guerilla territory, searching for spiritual liberty even as forces in the world relentlessly seek "to overthrow the freedom of all lands, nations, and countries." (Ether 8:25.)

New arrivals are not asked to renounce their country or that which is good in their culture. All must, however, let go of the things that injure the soul, and there are some such things in every life and in every culture.

When all these individuals have come from so great a distance to join the Church, surely we can go a second mile in friendshipping and fellowshipping them. If with quiet heroism they can cross the border into belief, surely we can cross a crowded foyer to extend the hand of fellowship. Has it been so long that we have forgotten our first anxious day at a new school or our timidity in a new town?

Many will come into the Church whose lives have been consistently righteous. They will have rejoicing without so much wrenching.

All arrivals, however, will need full and loving acceptance. Since priesthood leaders have determined that the newcomers' visas are in order, let us greet them genuinely, not with frowns and skepticism. It will be our job to lift them up, not to size them up. They will have known much rejection; now let them know much acceptance!

The Lord has said that the workers who come to His vineyard in the last hour will receive the same wages as old-timers. Likewise, oldtimers should not speak so much of the good old days but rather labor to bring even better days.

The story is told of the first two Marines in U.S. history, who served in the American Revolutionary War. One boarded a ship mere minutes ahead of the other. When the second man came on board, enthusiastic about being a Marine, the earlier arrival scornfully said, "You should have been here in the old outfit!"

Neither, said Paul, should we expect the social register to enter the Church en masse. (See 1 Corinthians 1:26.) Besides, a "Who's Who" is not needed in a church that teaches us all our real identity and in which there is, significantly, a democracy of dress in the holy temples.

Arrivals will come into the Church even as its leaders are being cruelly caricatured by some in the world. Imagine how television's six o'clock news would have portrayed Noah as he worked on his ark day after day. Actually, adversarial attention is merely a cruel form of commendation, if we can but stand the "praise."

Newcomers may even see a few leave the Church who cannot then leave the Church alone. Let these few departees take their brief bows in the secular spotlight; someday they will bow deeply before the throne of the Almighty, confessing that Jesus is the Christ and that this is His work. Meanwhile, let us not be surprised if, as the little stone seen by Daniel rolls relentlessly forth, some seek in vain to chip away at it.

Happily, among the hundreds of thousands of recruits will be mingled precious returnees who, like the prodigal son, have come to their senses. Filled with tender resolve, they too need a warm welcome. Let us emulate the father of the prodigal son who ran to greet his son while the son was still a great distance away, rather than waiting and then asking the son skeptically if he had merely come home to pick up his things!

Recruits and returnees should be candidly counseled by the lyrics of the hymn, "Think not, when ye gather to Zion" that all "your troubles and trials are through, . . . that all will be holy and pure . . . And confidence wholly secure: . . . [that] The Saints . . . have nothing to do but to look to your personal welfare and always be comforting you." (*Hymns*, no. 21.)

Let us involve newcomers quickly in the Lord's work. They have been called to His vineyard not just to admire but to perspire—not to "oh and aah," but to "hoe and saw." Let us make of them friends, not celebrities; colleagues, not competitors. Let us use their precious enthusiasm to beckon still others to come within the light.

Let us listen lovingly and encouragingly as all newcomers utter their first halting public prayers and give their first tender talks, feeling unready and unworthy—but so glad to belong. We can tell them, can we not, that the sense of inadequacy never seems to go away?

The Church is for the perfecting of the Saints, hence new arrivals are entitled to expect instant community but not instant sainthood—either in themselves or in others. It takes time and truth working patiently together "in process of time" to produce the latter in all of us. We are a people in process, to whom the Lord has said, "Zion must increase in beauty, and holiness." (D&C 82:14.)

What we now are as a people is not enough. All is not yet well in Zion. Now, as in the time of Alma, the bad conduct of a few members slows missionary work. (See Alma 39:11.) Indeed, Zion, the Lord has said, will be fully redeemed only after we have been first chastened. (D&C 100:13.) We must not be too long-suffering with our own shortcomings, however.

Those of us already in the kingdom are to give fresh evidence by the eloquence of our examples that we are committed to the calisthenics of daily improvement and not just to the rhetoric of eternal progression. Whether returnees or recruits, all must make that "mighty change" in their hearts, and this requires more than a slight change in our schedules.

The Lord has said of His laborers, "Blessed are they who shall seek to bring forth my Zion." (1 Nephi 13:37.) Seemingly ordinary people have been called to do extraordinary chores, and as we work, we notice each other's weaknesses. Hence all are urged to succor the weak, to lift up the hands which hang down, and to strengthen the feeble knees. (See D&C 81:5.) As we carry our much lighter crosses, we too stumble—only much more often.

If there are disappointments, let us not turn away from Zion; rather, let us remember Peter's immortal interrogative of the Savior, "Lord, to whom shall we go?" (John 6:68.) There is no other way out of this mortal maze, no other "plan of happiness." (Alma 42:8.)

Let all gospel instruction in the home or classroom be a genuine and mutual experience in learning—not doctrinal ping-pong. Let us both admire and respond to the honesty of those who may say, as did another new believer, "Lord, I believe; help thou mine unbelief"! (Mark 9:24.) Let us all understand, too, that those doctrines which may seem the most puzzling or the least attractive may well be those now most needed by us.

Let all of us be filled with quiet wonder, but also with quiet determination at the marvelous things we have been called to do. Nephi said, "For the Lord shall comfort Zion. . . . Joy and gladness shall be found therein, thanksgiving and the voice of melody." (2 Nephi 8:3.)

As we build a holier and a more beautiful Zion, with "the voice of melody" we will sing those lyrics—"All is well, all is well"—but at times as a reassuring sob as well as a song, awaiting the day Isaiah promised when such "sorrow and sighing shall flee away." (Isaiah 35:10.)

With Paul, we can say, "We are troubled on every side, yet not distressed; we are perplexed, but not in despair; Persecuted, but not forsaken; cast down, but not destroyed." (2 Corinthians 4:8-9.) Perhaps we can add, "We are challenged, but not surprised; we are falsely accused, but pray for our accusers; we are reviled, but are resplendent with Christian service."

The Savior will be in our midst. He will lead us along, saying, "Fear not, little flock" and urging us to do good even when we are badly done by. Indeed, we will find that putting off the natural man and becoming saintlike are both done best when we are in the company of and in cooperation with those who are doing likewise!

So it is that we find that the working out of our salvation is a day-by-day and deed-by-deed thing. Yes, there are moments that matter much more than others, including those in which a soul's salvation can be said to hang in the very balance. But even those big moments come into being because of the accumulation of small thoughts and small actions, such as a growing selfishness that causes an erring mother to leave a family in search of fulfillment. Regularized, mental fantasy may present, finally, a real choice between fidelity and breeching the seventh commandment.

But the big moment does not usually strike suddenly; when it comes, it is not so much a case of the first instance as more of a last chance—to reject with finality that which has massed ominously but gradually.

Accumulating righteousness, on the other hand, may not immunize us, but it strengthens us, for we can respond out of reflex without reprocessing, again and again, the same tired, old temptations.

There is great safety, therefore, in the day-to-day world, in our being careful about maintaining our spiritual environment and in doing our duties. It is not just a question of being kept too busy to sin grievously, though that is preferred to excessive leisure, but of our being freely and anxiously engaged because we are true believers. Therefore, the rejection of temptation by reflex is superior to agonizing any time—better to be practical than theatrical!

Hence there ought to be—as we regularly, even routinely, work out our salvation—a quiet sense of earned encouragement and of being a worthy laborer in the vast vineyard, perspiring but inspiring. A laborer who has put off the natural man is discernibly moving toward sainthood by becoming pure and spotless.

# 6

## *Being Pure and Spotless before God*

The interlocking and cross-supporting nature of God's commandments is everywhere noticeable. We cannot, for instance, have an eye single to the glory of God, thus keeping the first commandment, if we are of lustful eye in violation of the seventh commandment. Of course, purity is much more than sexual purity, but scriptural history shows—and contemporary times sadly reaffirm—that the adversary's largest harvest appears to come from this sector of sin. Special attention to the seventh commandment is needed as the Church expands in a hedonistic time.

There is a basic cluster of standards associated with chastity before marriage and fidelity after, all of which are a part of perhaps the least popular of the Ten Commandments. Keeping this commandment ("Thou shalt not . . . commit adultery, . . . nor do anything like unto it" [D&C 59:6]) will be—indeed is—a constant challenge in our time. Any individual weaknesses in this regard will surely be exploited by the adversary! Unlike physical afflictions that may, like Paul's, be given to us as a "thorn in the flesh," unchastity is a weakness of our own making. The Lord has said that He will succor us in times of temptation, but He will not indulge us. We can be sure, though we are given tempering weaknesses, that lust is not one of them.

89

Not a usual topic of ministerial sermons in our day, the seventh commandment is one of the least heeded but most needed laws of God. It is probably Exhibit A as to how much The Church of Jesus Christ of Latter-day Saints differs from many churches in the world on very basic behavioral issues. The world cares very little for the keeping of this commandment, as long as people appear to be admirable in any other respect. Violations of the seventh commandment are regarded by some as mere peccadilloes, and some writers almost gleefully report these lapses by past political heroes, telling us more about the writers than the heroes.

It is important for us to be philosophical defenders as well as practicers of chastity. Articulate advocacy is surely needed now to respond to some of the secular sophistry we see and hear in the world pertaining to immoral lifestyles.

Austin Farrer warned, "Though argument does not create conviction, the lack of it destroys belief. What seems to be proved may not be embraced; but what no one shows the ability to defend is quickly abandoned." (*Light on C.S. Lewis*, New York: Harcourt, Brace, and World, 1965, p. 26.) Peter said, "Be ready always to give an answer to every man that asketh you a reason of the hope that is in you with meekness and fear." (1 Peter 3:15.) Our personal hope for a better next world requires our keeping of the seventh commandment and encouragement to others to do likewise.

On national television recently a psychologist pushed the notion that, since the old ethics of our American society are no longer reconcilable with our present behavior, we ought to adjust our ethics downward, which recalled to this viewer another age and another advocate who pushed the carnally convenient notion that "whatsoever a man did was no crime." (Alma 30:17.)

This psychologist was saying, in effect, that because young people mature today at twelve, on the average, and don't marry, on the average, until they are twenty-two, the idea of abstaining from fornication or things "like unto it" is unrealistic. With the avoidance of pregnancy seemingly being the only real challenge for this psychologist, heavy petting was encouraged and all the things associated with it were seen as safe and practical substitutes.

Once they are driven off the high ground of moral principle, so many people are then forever falling back, trying to develop substitutes. Methadone replaces heroin—but the addiction remains. There will always be those who will think themselves quite clever for suggesting seeming ways out of such dilemmas, but their prescriptions are not "ways out" at all but, rather, "ways in"—into more carnal cul-de-sacs.

Moral uncertainty always leads to behavioral absurdity, and prescriptions that are value-free always prove finally to be so costly. Yet absurdity about immorality is achieving a certain momentum today.

As disciples, however, we cannot condone carnality just because it seems clever. We have been given the commandments and must walk in their light. We have even been instructed with regard to the perils of mental unchastity. (See Matthew 5:28.) The trends of a particular time cannot alter the eternal laws of God, nor can we give up just because there is a general giving way.

Another departure from the past that is touted by the world is pornography. Pornography first uses the oxygen of freedom to flourish and then proceeds to pollute the very atmosphere that made its existence possible in the first place. Industrial smelters are constrained—but smut shops flourish. There is no Environmental Protection Agency watching over the pornographic pollution that steadily settles into the marrow of a society made vulnerable by its spiritual valuelessness.

Deep inside some of the hardest doctrines (such as the seventh commandment) are truths and precious principles. Obedience to them actually brings both blessings *and additional knowledge*, as Peter promised. (See 2 Peter 1:8.)

For instance, Alma said that we must bridle all our passions so that we can be "filled with love." (Alma 38:12.) If such passions were actually true love, clearly they would not need to be replaced with true love. The Lord, in an 1839 revelation to the Prophet Joseph Smith, even linked our capacity to have "charity towards all men" (the second commandment) with our capacity to let virtue garnish our thoughts unceasingly. (See D&C 121:45.) If our mind is filled with wrong things, there will be no place in it for true love of God and our fellowmen.

Thus a failure to checkreign sensuality carries with it both personal penalties and, more than we realize, real deprivations for our peers and associates. No wonder Paul said that to feed these lusts is to "drown men in destruction." (1 Timothy 6:9.) Unchastity and sensuality are very preemptive in their demands.

In the parable of the sower, Jesus spoke of how some of those who might change for the better fail to do so because the lusts of former things actually "choke the word." (Mark 4:19.) Carnality is especially choking because it causes a profound contraction of the soul. As with the other commandments, disobeying means a shrinking of self, and obeying means an expanding of self.

In pondering the seventh commandment, we come to see, too, that we are also dealing with considerations of a transcendental or eternal character. In Proverbs we read,

"Whoso committeth adultery . . . *lacketh understanding*: he that doeth it destroyeth his own soul." (Proverbs 6:32. Italics added.) There are some consequences of sexual immorality that we are simply not able to measure fully, but they are, nevertheless, very real.

We are preparing now to live in a better world. If we are too quick to adapt to the ways of this fleeting and flawed world, that very adjustment will maladjust us for our life in the next. No wonder those who break this commandment are bereft of perspective and lack understanding.

There are, of course, some concerns associated with the seventh commandment that we share with the world. There is, for instance, a desire to avoid the *disease* that often goes with unchastity and infidelity. People naively assumed that with the coming of antibiotics, venereal disease would no longer be a concern. The secularists were blithely wrong again.

A second point of concurrence is avoiding pregnancies in unwed mothers. Unfortunately, when their pragmatism fails, the world's "final solution" is that Buchenwald for babies—abortion.

Ronald Butt wrote in the London *Times* (February 7, 1980): "For nearly 2,000 years of Christian civilization, taking the life of an unborn child was regarded as a vile and heinous moral offense which degraded humanity. When an abortion was done to save the life of the mother or to prevent a woman from the consequences of rape, those responsible, including the doctors, acted in consciousness that a grave moral decision was involved. Abortions to avoid illegitimate births, or otherwise for convenience, were performed with a secrecy that was as much the mark of the shame attaching to the deed as a consequence of its illegality." (As quoted in *Human Life Review*, Spring 1980, p.3.)

Abortion, like the unchastity about which Jacob so eloquently wrote, produces conditions in which many hearts die, "pierced with deep wounds." (Jacob 2:35.) Note the pain in these words to the author by a repentant, but still shaken, young woman who had had two abortions:

"I wonder about the spirits of those I have aborted—if they were there, if they were hurt. I was under three months each time, but a mother feels life before she feels movement.

"I wonder if they are lost and alone.

"I wonder if they will ever have a body.

"I wonder if I will ever have a chance again to bring those spirits back as mine."

A third gospel concern shared somewhat by the world is that sexual immorality assaults marriage and family life, further increasing the already spiraling divorce rate. Having so said, though, some in the world are not actually so concerned with family life. The prescience of Charles Peguy's assertion made earlier in this century is obvious that "the true revolutionaries of the twentieth century will be the fathers of decent and civilized families." (In John Lukacs, *The Passing of the Modern Age*, New York: Harper and Row, 1970, p. 82.)

Fortunately, the kingdom's reasons for keeping the seventh commandment include, but go far beyond, these three concerns, real as these concerns are.

The primary reason for obedience to all the laws of chastity is to keep the commandments of God. Joseph understood that reason clearly when he resisted the entreaties of Potiphar's predatory wife. Joseph, who clearly noted his loyalty to his employer, Potiphar, concluded, "How then can I do this great wickedness, and sin against God?" (Genesis 39:8-9.) Joseph's obedience was an act of many-splendored loyalty—to God, to himself, to his future family, to Potiphar, and, yes, even to Potiphar's wife, who lacked understanding.

Another major reason for complying is that breaking the seventh commandment costs us the companionship of the Holy Ghost, because He cannot abide in a sinful soul. This is an awful price that could be described only by those who have paid it. And without the Holy Ghost's help, we then become less useful, less perceptive, less functional, and less loving human beings. In a sense, we are then on the sick roll in the army of the Lord—and at that very time when we are so much needed at the front.

Sexual immorality is also dangerous because it is so desensitizing. Lasciviousness can, ironically, take people who wrongly celebrate their capacity to feel to a point where they lose their capacity to feel. They become, in the words of *three* different prophets in *three* different dispensations, "past feeling." (See 1 Nephi 17:45; Ephesians 4:19; Moroni 9:20.)

Norman Cousins warned: "People who insist on seeing everything and doing anything run the risk of feeling nothing. . . . Our highest responses are being blunted without our knowing it." ("See Everything, Do Everything, Feel Nothing," *Saturday Review*, January 23, 1971, p. 31.)

When we leave the light of each commandment, our perception of the real problem is blurred and our prescriptions are bound to be flawed. In no instance is the blurring more evident than with regard to the seventh commandment. For instance, there is grave concern, and with justified cause, about the abuse of prostitutes and the terrible problems of child prostitution and child pornography. One scarcely hears, however, any mention of keeping the seventh commandment in order to solve these dreadful problems—though it is the ultimate solution. The immediate retort is that since there are so many who do not hold with divine prescriptions or who are too weak to comply, other remedies are needed. Religious restraints are viewed as impractical! The keeping of the seventh commandment, however, would at once erase all the problems associated with prostitution, child prostitution, and pornography. Yet, the more distance societies place between themselves and the keeping of the seventh commandment, the larger and less manageable these problems become.

To assert that there is some way other than adherence to the divine standard that has come down to us through the centuries in our Judeo-Christian heritage is to introduce the inevitable rationalization that relativism always brings: if infidelity is not really wrong *per se*, then why cannot every individual walk "in his own way," determining that which pleases him or her and that which gives sensual pleasure— even if it be child molestation or masochism? A nonmoral ground is no ground at all! A pervert will be unimpressed by ethical relativism's norms. Besides, inner slackness finally dooms outer enforcement, for enforcement officials are not only dwarfed by the enormity of their tasks, but also become less effective as the definition of crime becomes less and less legally and behaviorally clear. One has only to pause and wonder about what the role of a vice squad would have been in Sodom and Gomorrah! The breaking of the seventh commandment was the beginning of the end even of Camelot.

In a society with declining tastes, standards will continue to be lowered as some new appetite or fashion makes its particular political thrust felt either by nonenforcement or in permissive legislation. Caesar, ever attuned to the roar of the crowd, is always ready to sanction the cry of another crowd even when it chooses a behavioral Barabbas.

To equate Eros with charity, the highest form of love, is to regard love mistakenly. The selfless atonement came through charity, not a lesser form of love. True love is the centerpiece attribute in both the first and second commandments—the attribute on which every other commandment and law hangs! Therefore, to misunderstand the true nature of love is to misunderstand life. To be unchaste, in the name of love, is to destroy something precious while pretending to celebrate its existence. Some say they are "for" love—but a rogue policeman is "for" law and order just as Benedict Arnold was "for" America.

Another of the consequences of gross sexual immorality with its desensitization is that it begins to rob man of hope. As an individual is emptied of hope, despair quickly enters in, for as one prophet said, "Despair cometh because of iniquity." (Moroni 10:22.) Thus wickedness and despair are terrifyingly self-reinforcing.

More than we know, the alienation abroad in the land is due in significant measure to the gross sexual immorality—before which faith, hope, and charity all fall, for that special triad of virtues is savaged by unchastity. Immorality enthrones selfishness, that implacable foe of charity.

There is some interesting mortal wisdom concerning this slackening of standards with regard to chastity and fidelity. This is cited not because we rely upon it for enunciatory truth, but because it is often necessary for us to speak to people after the manner of their understanding.

Charles Unwin, a British sociologist who labored at both Oxford and Cambridge, studied dozens of civilizations and was bold enough to forecast "in so many words that, in the struggle between nations, those who cling to chastity will, in all likelihood, keep the upper hand—last but not least, we shall add, because they try to keep intact the family which promiscuity and homosexuality (as well as the war between the sexes and the tension between the generations) tend to destroy." (*The Human Life Review*, Spring 1978, p. 71.) The French historian Ernest Renan said succinctly: "What gives one people the victory over another, who has it to a lesser degree, is chastity." (Ibid.)

John Lukacs observed that sexual immorality is at the very center of the moral crisis of our times—"it is not merely a marginal development." (*The Passing of the Modern Age*, New York: Harper & Row, 1970, p. 169.)

C. S. Lewis wrote: "When I was a youngster, all the progressive people were saying, 'Why all this prudery? Let us treat sex just as we treat all our other impulses.' I was simple-minded enough to believe they meant what they said. I have since discovered that they meant exactly the opposite. They meant that sex was to be treated as no other impulse in our nature has ever been treated by civilized people. . . . It is like having a morality in which stealing fruit is considered wrong—unless you steal nectarines." (Clyde S. Kibby, ed., *A Mind Awake: An Anthology of C. S. Lewis*, New York: Harcourt, Brace, and World, 1969, pp. 193-94.)

Lewis made an even more trenchant observation with regard to modern society's preoccupation with sex—and he did this before the titillation of TV talk shows, so many of which have merely transferred the language of the locker room to the living room. Such conversational shows are so often exercises in verbal voyeurism and would suggest, to a man from Mars, that earthlings have but a single concern.

Lewis wrote: "Now suppose you came to a country where you could fill a theatre by simply bringing in a covered plate onto a stage and then slowly lifting the cover so as to let every one see, just before the lights went out, that it contained a mutton chop or a bit of bacon, would you not think that in that country something had gone wrong with the appetite for food?" (*A Mind Awake*, pp. 194-95.)

When we lose our capacity to feel, it is because we have destroyed the tastebuds of the soul. We have blunted our capacity to appreciate the refinements, the graciousness, and the empathy that are needed here and that surely belong to that better world toward which we are pointed.

Our whole selfish society tends to travel light, pushing away from anyone who might be an obligation—jettisoning "used" friends, relatives, and even marriage partners. Disavowal and disposability are characteristic of the final stages of selfishness in which the individual is not willing to risk a commitment of any enduring nature nor to be depended upon for anything except the assertion of his appetites. Those souls whom sensuality has shrunken into ciphers constantly seek to erase their loneliness by sensations. But in the arithmetic of appetite, anything multiplied by zero still totals zero!

Failure to keep the seventh commandment also lowers self-esteem, because we are actually sinning against our divine nature and who we really are. (See 1 Corinthians 6:18-19.) And we are breeching promises made in the premortal world before we came here, promises that are imprinted, subtly but indelibly, on our soul.

Unchastity impacts severely on others in various ways. First, it suggests wrongly that everyone is, after all, the same; appetites will prevail and, therefore, one might as well join the march of the lustful lemmings now as later. It is too bad that those who are sexually immoral are not required to submit in advance an environmental impact statement before proceeding.

Second, just as our basic values are interactive, so are our basic institutions. We cannot corrupt our families and expect to have good governments! Once, for instance, we suggest by our behavior that the commandments do not really matter, then it is "open season." A parent may wink at embezzlement, his child at adultery, and his grandchild at treason.

Thus, these and other concerns about the seventh commandment go far beyond the world's concerns over disease and pregnancy.

The Church is constantly concerned with one of the ultimate dimensions of freedom that is freedom from sin. We share the world's concerns with political and economic freedom, the more visible and traditional dimensions of freedom. Paul said, however, "Where the Spirit of the Lord is, there is liberty." (2 Corinthians 3:17.) Jesus said, "The truth shall make you free." (John 8:32.) It is so easy to become imprisoned in the single well-lit cell of one impulse and one appetite.

When we think of this constellation of reasons, we can understand why it is not just recurring rhetoric when prophets like Moroni observe that the loss of chastity is the loss of that which is precious above all things. (See Moroni 9:9.) And why, so many times, the writers of the scriptures, observing their own people's decadence, have equated ripening in iniquity with the spread of fornication and adultery. (See Helaman 8:26.)

There is a last irony—but only for those who need it: The great apostle of love, John, reminded us that this world will pass away "and the lust thereof." (See 1 John 2:17.) This means, quite frankly, that not only can lust ruin this life, but it is also a pandering to an appetite that will have *no* existence at all in the next world!

If we had the full record of what happened at Sodom and Gomorrah, we would see this same cumulative giving way with each individual failure at each human intersection putting even more pressure on the remaining junctions until they too gave way.

Contrast all that happened in the decadent destroyed cities of the plain with that marvelous period of time when, at least for a few brief decades, there was a righteousness that did not lapse. There was a sweet Nephite society in which there were no whoredoms, nor any manner of lasciviousness, and "surely there could not be a happier people among all the people who had been created by the hand of God." (4 Nephi 1:16.)

Let us resist the rhetoric of the world and its conceptual caresses, and we will find that, if we stand fast, so will others—some surprisingly. Remember the lesson in the lines of Sadie Thompson in Somerset Maugham's story "Rain"? She said, after being disillusioned during a brief walk on the road to repentance, "You men, you filthy dirty pigs, you are all the same, all of you." Men are not all the same! Latter-day Saint men must act in such a way that women can experience that reality—just as Latter-day Saint women must be women of God, not of the world.

The seventh commandment has never contained more than a single standard!

Let us build our strong personal link in a chain of chastity and family fidelity, so it can proceed forth from grandparents to parents to children and then on to their posterity. To be so welded together is, of course, to be drawn together in the strongest kind of bond, and is to affirm, by our actions, that we believe in the commandments in spite of what is going on in the world around us.

Let us not company with fornicators—not because we

are too good for them, but, as C. S. Lewis wrote, because we are not good enough. Remember that bad situations can wear down even good people. Joseph had both good sense and good legs in fleeing from Potiphar's wife.

Moreover, along with the traditional predatory, selfish male there is now the "liberated," selfish female. Both, driven by appetite, have a false sense of being free—but it is, alas, the same sort of empty "freedom" Cain possessed (after he had broken the sixth commandment by slaying Abel) when, ironically, he said, "I am free." (Moses 5:33.)

Where mistakes have been made, remember that we have the glorious gospel of repentance. The miracle of forgiveness awaits all who are seriously sorry and who will follow the necessary steps. Bear in mind, however, that the breaking of the seventh commandment creates situations in which the soul must be scalded by shame, for only with real cleansing first can real healing occur.

When the impulse to do wrong appears, let us act against that impulse while the impulse is still weak and while the will is still strong. Dalliance merely means that the will weakens and the impulse grows stronger.

Since temptation and its thought patterns expand so as to fill the time made available, let us keep anxiously engaged in safe and good things. Idleness has a way of wrongly insisting, again and again, that it is ourselves we must think of pleasing.

Because our behavioral standards are different, we must come to despise the ridicule of the world. The scorn and derision of the world are fleeting. James, who was not shy concerning truth, counseled, "Ye adulterers and adulteresses, know ye not that the friendship of the world is enmity with God?" (James 4:4.)

Those who are in error must not call the cadence for our

lives, for those who boast of their sexual conquests are only boasting of that which has conquered them—in the same way that drinkers who make nervous jokes about drunkenness are only mocking that which has come to mock them. We may pity behavioral clones, but we do not envy them.

In our concern for justice, let us, therefore, deal justly with ourselves. There is a very telling verse in the Book of Mormon that describes an ancient political leader with these words: "He did do justice unto the people, but not unto himself because of his many whoredoms." (Ether 10:11.) This verse presents the paradox we often see in secular leaders. William Law, seventeenth century writer, in writing of a lady of some renown, said of her that she was "nice in everything that concerned her body or dress, careless of everything that might benefit her soul."

Thus some of the sad consequences attached to that immorality which breeches the seventh commandment are: penicillin instead of abstinence; pills instead of children; transient partners instead of marriage; childbirth with unwed parents; old perversions masquerading as new thrills —and all of it soaked in alcohol.

As far as the stern but sweet seventh commandment is concerned, *obedience is also entrance.* By avoiding the evils and consequences of unchastity, we also gain entrance and access to such blessings as always accompany those who keep the commandments. Moses promised ancient Israel that if they would keep the commandments, certain blessings would come on them and overtake them. (Deuteronomy 28:2.) These next blessings and others shall come on us and overtake us if we keep the seventh commandment.

Keeping the stern seventh commandment, in the full sense, yields the blessings of serenity through our being in harmony with divine law and the Lord—an immensely important blessing in this age of alienation. Obedience likewise gives the blessing of vivid identity through our being in harmony with our own potential selfhood. The gospel helps us think of ourselves not only for what we now are, but for what we have the power to become.

Keeping the seventh commandment brings the blessing of specific and deserved self-esteem. How many neighbors go unloved because so many people thus despise themselves?

The keeping of this commandment blesses us with freedom from the tyranny of appetite, which may be the most oppressive tyranny of all.

There comes the blessing of freedom from corrosive guilt with its wasted rationalizations and self-pity.

We come to know the blessing of expanded free agency by learning to act wisely for ourselves rather than merely being acted upon by appetite, a vital dimension of agency. (2 Nephi 2:26.)

There is too the significant blessing of personal momentum that always comes when we practice decision making in which we both *reject wrong* and *choose the good*. We thus avoid what one prophet called the in-betweenness of the "sorrowing of the damned." (Mormon 2:13.) It is not enough to reach a bland behavioral point when we no longer take pleasure in sin; we must hunger and thirst for righteousness.

Additionally, there is the immensely important blessing of the integrity of soul, which leads to personal wholeness and unafraid openness. How can we, for instance, become "one flesh" in marriage if, as we enter into marriage, we are sundered and several selves? Chastity, integrity, and serenity—these are interdependent and inexpressible blessings that come from purity and charity.

Therefore, part of being a true believer is to keep the seventh commandment, for "the commandment is a lamp" and the true believer walks by the light of the lamp. He knows he dare not do otherwise, for it is only by that light that he sees his remaining spots and can continue the scrubbing of the soul!

# 7

## *True Believers in Christ*

Perhaps it is the very simplicity of the Christ-centered life—being "true believers in Christ"*—that makes it such a difficult subject to discuss. Its requirements, while not nominal, are actually quite simple: Keep His commandments! The true believer, notwithstanding his weaknesses, is faithfully underway even though he may feel overwhelmed at times; he is a causal Christian, not a casual one, and therein lies some of the challenge.

The Prophet Joseph Smith said we need to know that the "course of life" we are pursuing "is according to the will

---

*In our time the words "true believer" have come to connote intense, mindless robots who are part of political mass movements in which individuals, among other things, seek to escape from the burdens of freedom. However, even in view of this connotational concern, reflecting our age and time, the phrase used by the apostle Nephi (and earlier by Alma) is too precious not to bring to the fore. Besides, there are some sobering parallels. The Christians who were called "true believers" were, in Book of Mormon times, faithful members of the Church who had taken upon themselves the name of Christ "gladly." (See Alma 46:15.) They were persecuted by the disbelievers and irreligionists of their time because of their commitment to Christ and because of their humility. Yet they did not strike back. (See Nephi 1:29-37.) The Three Nephites were numbered among the "true believers." It was also a time when there was a "great division among the people" (A.D. 231).

of God, in order to . . . exercise faith in him unto life and salvation." (Lectures on Faith 6:1.) Obviously, our imperfections make God's full and final approval of our lives impossible now, but the correctness of the basic course of our life can be known notwithstanding our weaknesses. If we have that basic reassurance, we can then further develop our faith and give needed attention to pacing and to overcoming our weaknesses.

Happily, there are various and specific duties in our course of life that go with (and help us to keep) the basic commandments. These duties are to be done, one by one, without doubting their eventual value, just as farmers do not agonize over every seed they plant. These duties are usually quite measurable and quite familiar; they include partaking of the sacrament, receiving the gospel ordinances, attending meetings and the temple, praying, fasting, studying the scriptures, rendering Christian service, attending to all family duties, being involved in missionary work and reactivation, doing genealogical work, paying our tithes and offerings, and being temporally prepared. The true believer gladly does these things and sees their connection to the commandments.

These enumerated duties are, of course, not particularly glamorous. Yet they are practical and specific expressions of the keeping of the first two great commandments—love of God and love of neighbor. For instance, proper participation in the Lord's welfare program carries with it this significant blessing: "And now, for the sake of these things which I have spoken unto you—that is, *for the sake of retaining a remission of your sins from day to day*, that ye may walk guiltless before God—I would that ye should *impart of your substance to the poor. . . .* " (Mosiah 4:26. Italics added.)

However, because most of us have considerable difficulty moving from basic truths and principles to the practical application of the same, one of the functions that church duties perform (and, even on occasion, church programs) is to help us make that linkage. True enough, the highly developed disciple will have no difficulty translating his devotion to the Savior into loving his neighbor.

He will find a hundred wonderful ways to neighbor. But most of us need some urging and some guiding, so that we understand, for instance, that one part of keeping the second commandment is to share the gospel of Jesus Christ with our neighbor.

It is accurate to say also that, when we are living well enough, the promptings of the Spirit will guide us in tactical matters (telling us all things we should do [see 2 Nephi 32:3]). Once we really know the "what" and the "why," the "how" will become clear. But, once again, there is a transition to be made in which each of us can be helped if we are presented with implementing duties and suggestions. For instance, deliberate decisions must be made in order to achieve that desirable condition, "love at home," such as budgeting enough time at home to, among other things, express love to children by adding to their storehouse of happy memories. Singing that song is not enough; it must be matched by wise scheduling to benefit the family, which is often victimized by our busyness.

The danger, therefore, is very real if we merely presume that discipleship represents mental assent to behavioral abstracts, when what is needed is for us to be drawn by small duties toward the fulfillment of the two great and challenging commandments. We cannot become true believers in Christ merely by keeping the sixth commandment—thou shalt not kill!

Significantly, of the Ten Commandments, *as originally stated*, eight were stated as prohibitions and two were stated as affirmations. (See Exodus 20:1-17; Deuteronomy 5:6-21; Leviticus 19:18.) Jesus' restatement cast the two great commandments in a grand affirmative. (See Matthew 22:34-40.)

The commandments that require us to *do* rather than to *abstain* are precisely those concerning which we often need the most help. Our duties especially help us because they are usually the "thou shalts"!

Even so, we do not wish to be driven by quotas into doing temple endowments or into achieving convert baptisms. At the same time, the absence of any exhortation at all concerning our duties finds most of us not too likely to go to the temple or to be suitably active in member-missionary work.

Thus it is that we are left, if we are not careful, in a very interesting posture: we are aware of the prohibitions such as "Thou shalt not steal" in which we abstain from certain actions, but we are not necessarily propelled by these abstentions onward to the affirmative actions necessary to keep such commandments as the fourth commandment (remembering the Sabbath day) or the fifth (honoring father and mother).

We do not generally have much trouble envisioning what is meant by coveting a neighbor's wife. We may need some help as to how broad and comprehensive the ninth commandment (bearing false witness) actually is, but at least we can envision specific things that are prohibited.

With regard, however, to the commandments that require affirmative deeds on our part, we are, quite frankly, not always sufficiently understanding of the various ways in which those commandments are to be kept. We understand that we cannot keep the second commandment —loving our neighbor as ourselves—if we steal from him, violating the eighth commandment. But do we understand that keeping the second commandment would include helping a neighbor who is "different" to be accepted in the neighborhood just as we would wish to be?

The duties, tasks, and callings given to us are opportunities not only to keep the prohibitory commandments, but are also significant and needed in helping to make the affirmations required in keeping all the commandments.

We may not feel that we need reminders all of the time, for as we grow and develop, a reminder of how we have truly progressed will become less and less necessary—but only in that particular thing. Few of us are generally so far along that we do not need these reminders. Furthermore, the duty least enjoyed, like the doctrine least understood, may be the one most needed now.

Great care must be exercised so that, as leaders and members, we do not pass off our personal preferences as the Lord's principles; we must not confuse our religious hobbies with His orthodoxy! There is a difference between a spiritual impression and a personal obsession. The latter may merely mask a long-held drive to be heard or to be vindicated, and aging does not automatically improve such views.

Likewise, church duties must be kept simple as befits the basic commandments that the various duties help us to keep. We must not evolve the ecclesiastical equivalent of the "laws of the Medes and Persians." The latter happened once before and brought the deserved reproof of the original Lawgiver!

The Church, therefore, is in the interesting position of having to recommend a curricular and program "diet" for a whole people rather than for just one hungry family, and this without knowing for sure how many will sit down at a given meal or the precise form of their needs.

The repetition and the insistence may at times irritate us, unless we remember why it is that it must be so. In such a circumstance, it is foolish for one to depend entirely upon others to see his every need. Too much dependency will not move us forward spiritually, hence the importance of individual and family gospel study.

When, therefore, we are making progress in our effort to be righteous, we need and deserve some reassurance and encouragement rather than the sense of being perpetually inadequate. At the same time, we must not be irritated at the reminders that there are yet more things to be done. Sometimes in the midst of this duality of pulls upon us, there are those who unwisely take refuge in speaking of the commandments in large, macromorality terms, disdaining the tactical duties. Others, alas, lose themselves in the few duties they prefer and shun the balanced development that a true believer achieves.

The true believer, moreover, knows that even within each commandment there are unfolding dimensions. We are, for instance, not only to avoid committing adultery physically as prohibited by the seventh commandment, but, as Jesus taught, we are also to avoid committing adultery mentally. (See Matthew 5:28.) We are not merely to attend the temple mechanically to do the work for our dead, but when we go, we ought also to meditate and contemplate, perhaps having spiritual experiences there while at the same time we are doing what may seem to be a rather routine duty.

Thus the level of our compliance with the commandments is, like it or not, a many-dimensional thing. We are most apt to achieve quality compliance when, in fact, we are "meek and lowly of heart" and are ready to be taught things we may not have even known existed! One of the great virtues of the meek is that they are not easily offended by counsel and suggestions. Nor are the lowly in heart inclined to see themselves as "above all that." The seemingly routine duties of discipleship must not be approached on the basis of "I've done that before," as if God were required to supply us with new thrills. Mortality has been described as being like working a vineyard—never as a day at a carnival. When we are involved developmentally, we are not merely "cheerleaders" but are "players" on the field of life, for *believing* always takes the form of *doing* as well as *thinking*. Indeed, we could not be true believers in Christ if we shunned doing the chores of His kingdom.

When we perform these measurable duties properly and for the right reason, this produces a series of highly desirable outcomes that are less measurable but very real. Our prayerful performance is consecrated by the Lord for our good and the welfare of our souls (see 2 Nephi 32:9); what is consecrated is our real growth, not the froth and flash of the periodic performer.

Indeed, we will even find that when we have personal, reinforcing spiritual experiences, they will almost always occur in the course of our carrying out the specific duties named above.

Further, carrying out these duties will entitle us to an ever-increasing companionship of the Holy Ghost. And when we have the Spirit with us, it means we have achieved significant Christ-centeredness in our lives, for we cannot be close to one member of the Godhead without being close to all three.

Significantly, when President Brigham Young experienced having the Prophet Joseph Smith appear to him in February 1847, President Young asked the Prophet if he had a message. The Prophet "very earnestly" said: "Tell the people to be humble and faithful, and be sure to keep the Spirit of the Lord and it will lead them right. Be careful and not turn away the still small voice; it will teach you what to do and where to go; it will yield the fruits of the Kingdom. . . . " (*Manuscript History of Brigham Young*, February 23, 1847.) Of the many things the Prophet might have said, this was his message.

Similarly, when President Wilford Woodruff was visited by President Brigham Young about two years after the latter's death, President Woodruff asked President Young if he had a message for the Saints in Arizona. President Young said, "Tell the people to get the Spirit of the Lord and keep it with them." The similar content of the messages is not surprising, but it is, nevertheless, striking.

Doing correct deeds produces correct (and reassuring) feelings, including having the Spirit. President David O. McKay said, for instance, that with spirituality we will have a "consciousness of victory over self"; we will feel our "faculties unfolding" and "truth expanding the soul," not unlike the swelling seed analogy in Alma 32. (*Treasures of Life*, Deseret Book Co., 1962, p. 437.)

No wonder Alma said it is not enough for us to have once been close to the Savior—so was Sidney Rigdon! We may once have "felt to sing the song of redeeming love," but "can [we] feel so now?" (Alma 5:26.)

President McKay said of the spirituality that characterizes the true believer that it "impels one to conquer difficulties"—it causes a leaning into life, not away from it. This actuating instead of passive posture fits with what the prophet Nephi said about the importance of acting wisely

for ourselves in life and not merely waiting to be acted upon. (See 2 Nephi 2:26.) Indeed, a willingness to conquer difficulties is essential, since Jesus' disciples are sometimes
given "thorns in the flesh"—even when there are no apparent rose gardens!

The Christ-centered life also produces in us not a "woe-
ful countenance," but the much-needed ingredient of a dis-
ciplined enthusiasm to work righteousness. We need this
quality, week after week and day after day, as we meet
with and try to help people who "droop in sin." (2 Nephi
4:28.) The electricity of our enthusiasm for righteousness
can help to brace and straighten them. With this enthusiasm for righteousness, we also avoid the feeling of being
plateaued in our own progress, for new adventures are seldom initiated when we are in repose.

Our Christian duties are like keys on a piano keyboard:
touch them correctly and in concert and renewing music is
inevitable; if one chord doesn't lift us, another will! But one
must do the touching himself, for we are not dealing with a
player piano.

Personal progress and drawing closer to the Savior require our trusting not only in the Lord's plan for all mankind, but especially trusting in His unfolding and particularized plan for each of us. Drawing ever closer to the Lord
and becoming a true believer, therefore, means much more
than merely acknowledging that He is in charge, though
that is a beginning. Even believers who remain under-
involved with Him are, in a sense, living without Him in
the world. Alma's warning that living without God in the
world is "contrary to the nature of happiness" (Alma 41:11)
was not just for agnostics!

The real test is (and always has been), "How much do
we love Him?" We know how much He loves us. His test

is, "If ye love me, keep my commandments." (John 14:15.)

We may say quite sincerely and even somewhat accurately that we are doing reasonably well at commandment keeping. Let us ponder, however, the episode with the young man who told the Savior that he too had kept the commandments from his youth. Jesus then gave him an added and very customized challenge: to go and sell all that he had and give the proceeds to the poor and then "take up the cross, and follow me." Doing this, said the Savior to the young man, would take care of the "one thing thou lackest." (Mark 10:21.) For some of us, would that it were just one thing! But having a healthy consciousness of that which we yet lack can become an additional test and spur. Though we may have already proved we can play checkers, are we now ready to play chess? Are we willing to let the Lord lead us into further developmental experiences? Or do we shrink back? The things that "greatly enlarge the soul" have no part with shrinking!

What follow are some useful tactical tests to help us measure how we are doing in developing the spirituality that characterizes the true believer in Christ.

1. True spirituality helps us to achieve balance between being too content with our present self and the equally dangerous human tendency we might have of wishing for more enlarged and impactful roles. Alma said, "But behold, . . . I ought to be content with the things which the Lord hath allotted unto me." However, note the often-ignored, but tutoring, verse that follows: "Now, seeing that I know these things, why should I desire more than to perform the work to which I have been called?" (Alma 29:3.) To develop that kind of justifiable contentment—to better use our existing opportunities—is obviously one of our challenges, particularly so when we seem to be in a

"flat" period of life. We may feel underused, under-whelmed, and underappreciated even though we are ig-noring unused opportunities for service all about us.

2. Are there some Jethros in our lives to give us needed and sometimes hard counsel?

"And Moses' father in law said unto him, The thing that thou doest is not good. Thou wilt surely wear away, both thou, and this people that is with thee: for this thing is too heavy for thee; thou art not able to perform it thyself alone." (Exodus 18:17-18.)

Do we have Jethros who can speak to us with loving di-rectness and yet be received humbly by us?

Further, since a Jethro may be anywhere, do we listen "down" and "sideways" as well as "up"?

"And [Naaman's] servants came near, and spake unto him, and said, My father, if the prophet had bid thee do some great thing, wouldest thou not have done it? how much rather then, when he saith to thee, Wash, and be clean?" (2 Kings 5:13.)

Naaman did not overlook "underlings." Furthermore, he was cleansed because he did not persist in his rejection of seeming routine.

3. Does a sense of proportion and discernment govern our choices, so that our Martha-like anxieties do not make the Mary-like choices less and less likely?

"And Jesus answered and said unto her, Martha, Mar-tha, thou art careful and troubled about many things: But one thing is needful: and Mary hath chosen that good part, which shall not be taken from her." (Luke 10:41-42. See also 38-40.)

We can be conscientious but still be confused about our priorities. How we spend our time is at least as good a measure of us as how we spend our money. An inventory of how we spend our disposable time will tell us where our treasure is. (Matthew 6:19-21.)

4. Are our personal prayers the easy and casual petitions—like one of Oliver Cowdery's concerning which the Lord said, "Behold, you have not understood; you have supposed that I would give it unto you, when you took no thought save it was to ask me" (D&C 9:7)—or have we moved on at least some of the time to inspired petitions, prayers of the high quality that the Lord said we could, one day, utter?

"And if ye are purified and cleansed from all sin, ye shall ask whatsoever you will in the name of Jesus and it shall be done. But know this, it shall be given you what you shall ask." (D&C 50:29-30.)

"He that asketh in the Spirit asketh according to the will of God; wherefore it is done even as he asketh." (D&C 46:30.)

The Lord said commendingly to a true believer in another age: "And now, because thou hast done this with such unwearyingness, behold, I will bless thee forever; and I will make thee mighty in word and in deed, in faith and in works; yea, even that all things shall be done unto thee according to thy word, for thou shalt not ask that which is contrary to my will." (Helaman 10:5.)

5. Do we have both right conduct and right reasons for that conduct? Are we so secure in our relationship with the Lord that our goodness and attention to duty would continue even if it were not seen of men? Would we fill our roles in the Church even if there were no mortal taking of the roll?

"Take heed that ye do not alms before men, to be seen of them: otherwise ye have no reward of your Father which is in heaven." (Matthew 6:1.)

"We then that are strong ought to bear the infirmities of the weak, and not to please ourselves." (Romans 15:1.)

"Not with eyeservice, as men-pleasers; but as the servants of Christ, doing the will of God from the heart." (Ephesians 6:6.)

6. When, professionally or associationally, or even in Church service, we seem to have been "put out to pasture," can we still say gladly and gratefully of the Lord (and mean it), "He maketh me to lie down in green pastures"? (Psalm 23:2.) The green coloring in plant life comes from chlorophyll, and it occurs only in the presence of light. Likewise, the greenness of the opportunities all around us in our present pastures are fully seen only in the glow of the gospel light.

7. When we are misrepresented, misquoted, or misused, do we still love and pray sincerely for those who despitefully use us? Can we forgive them lest the greater sin remain in us?

8. When someone seems to surpass us spiritually and does "our thing" even better than we, can we genuinely rejoice and give them heartfelt and sincere praise and sustain them? Can we not come to understand that God's perfect love for each of us is eternal and unchanging and that He has prepared a place for each of us which, if we are righteous, will not be given to another? Against that promise, how important are mortal organization charts?

9. Can we truly remember that forgetting is a specific dimension of forgiving? It is Lordlike—"I [will] remember [their sins] no more." (D&C 58:42.) Do we really help others to get deservingly reclassified? How recently have we reclassified someone?

Let our generosity greet and reassure the repentant and, likewise, beckon the almost-repentant whose pride warily and anxiously probes the quality of our fellowship and the possibility of forgiveness.

Can we, to use Alma's phrase, "give place" for the spiritual growth of others? Are we truly ready to receive not only the repentant, but also the frail who have grown strong? In the City of God, there will be lots of "new kids on the block"!

10. Do we trust the Lord enough not only to cope with, but also to use, seeming deprivation? to see opportunity within tragedy as did Joseph anciently? After Jacob's death, Joseph's brothers were frightened once again, fearing revenge because of what they had done to Joseph so many years before. Joseph simply said to them, "But as for you, ye thought evil against me; but God meant it unto good, to bring to pass, as it is this day, to save much people alive." (Genesis 50:20.) Surely we, among all mankind, should be patient in seeming tragedy, trusting the Lord and doing our duties while things unfold.

11. Are we growing in our patience? The Lord has said of certain challenges: "These things remain to overcome through patience, that such may receive a more exceeding and eternal weight of glory." (D&C 63:66.)

Paul stated: "Wherefore seeing we also are compassed about with so great a cloud of witnesses, let us lay aside every weight, and the sin which doth so easily beset us, and let us run with patience the race that is set before us." (Hebrews 12:1.)

Furthermore, patiently following the living prophets is vital, whereas trying to get ahead of the Brethren is a sure way of falling behind.

12. Finally, are we ready to follow the Lord into soul-stretching experiences, "to move forward," as President David O. McKay said, "to conquer our difficulties," even if

it means having experiences in which we are schooled through suffering, just as Jesus learned through suffering? In a stunning declaration, Alma spoke of Jesus and His atonement and of how even the Savior learned certain things "according to the flesh":

"And he shall go forth, suffering pains and afflictions and temptations of every kind; and this that the word might be fulfilled which saith he will take upon him the pains and the sicknesses of his people.

"And he will take upon him death, that he may loose the bands of death which bind his people; and he will take upon him their infirmities, that his bowels may be filled with mercy, according to the flesh, *that he may know according to the flesh how to succor his people according to their infirmities.*" (Alma 7:11-12. Italics added.)

Jesus, being sinless, could not have known suffering caused by sin—but the agonies of the atonement made it possible for Christ to succor us in our weaknesses and infirmities!

You and I on a much lesser scale may also need to undergo certain experiences "according to the flesh" in order to increase our capacity to help other people, bringing experiences we may not want, but which the Lord in His wisdom may insist upon.

These words from a sobering, sweet letter written by a gallant but modest student at Brigham Young University attest to a significant spirituality in one so young:

I have now had leukemia diagnosed for fifteen months, although few people even know about it. My goal has been to lead as normal a life as is possible; hence, the subject rarely gets mentioned because most people I have encountered, doctors included, tend to treat it as a tragedy rather than as an incentive to get one's affairs in order promptly.

My parents took the news quite hard, perhaps because my brother died unexpectedly eleven years ago of undiagnosed causes. Most are pessimistic; however, I have failed to see how pessimism would help me make the best use of my time, which is of an unknown length, not only for me, but for everyone.

Against medical and parental advice, I have since gotten married and am finishing my first year at BYU and we're expecting a baby in July. I feel great and am truly enjoying the blessings that are coming from being married in the temple, studying the scriptures, working hard in school, and living each day rather than simply waiting to die as some would recommend.

Fifteen months ago, my then fiance and I thought that if I could live long enough just for us to be sealed, that was all we would ask for. Therefore, we consider everything since then a great gift from the Lord. We still dream and plan for a long family life together, and it gives to us a certain comfort to know that our situation is in the Lord's hands and is not bound by man's limitations.

13. Are we anxiously engaged in bringing and retaining new converts in the fold? (See chapter 5.) Or are missionary and reactivation work something in which we merely serve as spectators?

14. Can we rejoice in the many blessings we now have without brooding over those that are temporarily withheld from us? What we do not have must not be allowed to spoil what we do have.

15. Are we careful about giving offense or causing others to stumble?

In a story about the city of Enoch a few years ago, a character in the story said in a letter to a friend some things about the way in which shortcomings add to the stress of others:

Not only do we gain greater happiness ourselves when we are righteous, but we also help our neighbor in subtle ways. How often the weaknesses in one man become a temptation to another man! My de-

sire for wealth and gems can cause another man's envy; my temper
has, at times past, dissolved your patience. One man's incontinence
destroys what little is left of a righteous woman's resolve. One person's
lust becomes another's way to wealth. A man's drunkenness becomes
another man's excuse for sabbath-breaking to enlarge his vineyards.
(Neal A. Maxwell, *Of One Heart*, Deseret Book, 1975, p. 28.)

Whatever the list of tactical tests contains concerning
regular, personal improvement in our lives, however, we
are best advised to consult our conscience. We should not
take on too many projects all at once, lest we fail at all of
them. Furthermore, it is best to concentrate on betterment
in the basics, even if at first the pace seems somewhat slow.
Each success will increase our self-esteem and further en-
hance our capacity to love and to help others.

Along with such attributes and qualities already noted,
the true believer in Christ may be further characterized.

He is innocent as to sin, but he is not naive about worldly things. Neither is he offended by the simplicity of the
Lord's way. He knows too that His constancy does not
mean monotony, but high adventure

He is harmless because he keeps the second commandment. But he is powerful because of his righteousness, for
his righteousness permits him to access the powers of
heaven, which cannot be handled in any other way.

He is serious about the living of his life, but he is happy
and of good cheer. His humor is the humor of hope and his
mirth is the uplifting mirth of morality, not the cutting cleverness of despair. Let the kaleidoscope of life's circumstances be shaken, again and again, and the "true believer
in Christ" will still see, "with the eye of faith," divine design, purpose, and pattern in his life.

Like his Master, the true believer loves his life but is
willing to lay it down or to see it slip slowly away through

affliction. In the midst of such affliction, however, like Job, he will not "charge God foolishly." If he is given a "thorn in the flesh," he will not demand to see the rose garden.

His love makes no parade, yet his light has become more than a little one. He is still imperfect but is visibly becoming less so.

He understands the difference between ends and means; that some Church aids are, in a sense, scaffolding for the soul; and that such scaffolding one day will be removed like waterwings or training wheels.

The true believer is kind but candid. He is tolerant of others but is ever willing to confront himself with the need for improvement.

He understands that the ultimate freedoms are freedom from sin and freedom from death. He is exceedingly grateful for God's gift of agency, but freely submits, childlike, to his Father in heaven. He understands the difference between being childlike and childish.

He is humble enough to "serve tables," but is sensible enough to share his time and talent on the basis of priorities—doing the things of most worth.

There is a regalness about the true believer in Christ, however humble in appearance he may be. The light of Christ that is in him is often discernible, and his love is felt unmistakably by others. The true believer's *cris de coeur* is heard not so much over the tragedies as the world measures tragedies, for his cry of the heart comes because of the tragedy of sin, because he sees things as they really are— not only what is, but lamentably what might have been.

He is settled in his soul; even in the midst of war and tumult, if he lives, he lives unto the Lord, and if he dies, he dies unto the Lord.

Unlike those who have a flamboyant devil-*may*-care

124                                    *Notwithstanding My Weakness*

lifestyle, his is the quiet and assured heaven-*does*-care attitude.

The true believer can read the depressing signs of the times without being depressed, because he has a particularized and "perfect brightness of hope," and he knows that Christ will lift him up. (See Moroni 9:25.) He does not naively depend on the actions or decisions of mortal rulers and assemblies, congresses, or parliaments to lift him up, though he is grateful for any true success by these. As Joseph Smith observed: "The laws of men may guarantee to a people protection in the honorable pursuits of this life, and the temporal happiness arising from a protection against unjust insults and injuries; and when this is said, all is said, that can be in truth, of the power, extent, and influence of the laws of men, exclusive of the law of God." (*Teachings of the Prophet Joseph Smith*, p. 50.)

Besides, the true believer knows that in the awful winding-up scenes, human deterioration will be finally and decisively met by Divine intervention.

The true believer knows, however, that Christ's glorious return will be preceded by much misery. But then the darkness will be broken by a millennial dawn and endless day. He understands, therefore, that the sooner he renounces the world, the sooner he can help to save some in it. Such an individual is the true believer in Christ!

Therefore, let us become such and proceed to make our way, righteously and resolutely, notwithstanding our weaknesses, to the beckoning City of God. There the self-assigned gatekeeper is Jesus Christ, who awaits us out of a deep divine desire to *welcome* us as much as to *certify* us; hence, "He employeth no servant there." (2 Nephi 9:41.) If we acknowledge Him now, He will lovingly acknowledge and gladly admit us then!

# Index

Tragedy, seeing opportunity in, 119

Ultimate hope, 50
Unbelief, results of, 38
Unchastity, 92

"Vanity Fair," 37, 74

Washington, George, 21-22
Weak things to break down the mighty, 12
Weaknesses, awareness of, 12-13; God's love overcomes, 22-23

Weariness, counsel on, 3
Williams, Frederick G., 14
Willingness, 56
Woman, "liberated," 102
Woodruff, Wilford, 113

Young, Brigham, quotation from, 28; saw Joseph Smith in vision, 113; appeared to Wilford Woodruff in vision, 113

Zion, building, 87
Zion's Camp, 11